Unshakable:

Pillars of Godly Womanhood

(Pillars of Faith That Changed History)

Gerard Assey

Unshakable:
Pillars of Godly Womanhood
(Pillars of Faith That Changed History)

By
Gerard Assey

Published by:
Gerard Assey
19/18, Palli Arasan Street
Anna Nagar East
Chennai - 600 102

ISBN: 978-81-985691-3-4

Table of Contents

Preface

Throughout history, women have played a pivotal role in God's grand design—women of courage, wisdom, faith, and perseverance who stood firm in the face of trials and became pillars of unshakable godliness. Some were queens and leaders, others were humble servants, mothers, or outcasts, but all had one thing in common: they encountered the living God and were forever transformed.

"Unshakable: *Pillars of Godly Womanhood* (Pillars of Faith That Changed History)" is a journey through the lives of such women—women whose faith changed history. From the Old Testament to the New Testament, we meet those who trusted God in the waiting, persisted in prayer, served with excellence, and boldly declared the gospel. Their stories are not distant, ancient tales; they are living testimonies that still echo into our present day, reminding us that God is looking for faithful, willing vessels through whom He can work mightily.

As you turn these pages, you will walk alongside Hannah, whose prayers gave birth to a prophet; Elizabeth, who remained steadfast in waiting; Mary Magdalene, whose devotion led her to be the first witness of the Resurrection; Lydia, a successful businesswoman who used her resources for the gospel; Priscilla, who taught and discipled alongside her husband—and many more. Their lives are blueprints of what it means to be a pillar of faith in a world that often seeks to shake our foundation.

This book is not just about history; it is about you. The same God who called these women calls you today. The same faith that strengthened them is available to you now. Whether you are a mother raising godly children, a leader in your church, a businesswoman using your success for God's glory, or someone searching for purpose, this book will encourage you to embrace your divine calling with boldness and confidence.

At the end of each chapter, you will find reflection questions to help you apply these lessons to your own journey. This is not just a book to read—it is a book to experience. My prayer is that as you go through these pages, God will stir within you a deep conviction to rise as a pillar of godly womanhood, standing firm in faith, unshakable in your calling, and unwavering in your love for Him.

Are you ready to embrace the legacy of faith that has changed history?

Then let's begin.

The Divine Design of Womanhood

In the grand narrative of creation, woman was never an afterthought. She was not an accident, nor a mere addition to complete the story of man. She was an intentional, masterfully designed creation of God—formed, not from the dust like Adam, but from his very rib, signifying deep connection, partnership, and purpose. The divine fingerprint upon womanhood is undeniable, and its significance reverberates through the pages of Scripture and history.

Understanding God's Original Purpose for Women

Genesis 1:27-28 declares, *"So God created mankind in His own image, in the image of God He created them; male and female He created them. God blessed them and said to them, 'Be fruitful and increase in number; fill the earth and subdue it.'"* From the very beginning, God created women with equal dignity, value, and purpose alongside men. She was designed to reflect His image, to steward His creation, and to play a critical role in the unfolding of His divine plan.

The misconception that woman was merely made to serve man is far from the biblical truth. When God created Eve, He called her a *"helper"* (ezer) (Genesis 2:18). The Hebrew word ezer is the same word used to describe God as Israel's helper in times of trouble (Psalm 33:20, Deuteronomy 33:26). This means that a woman's role is one of strength, support, and partnership, not inferiority. She was called to stand alongside man as a warrior in God's kingdom, fulfilling her role with wisdom, grace, and divine purpose.

Throughout Scripture, we see women fulfilling powerful roles: prophets, judges, queens, intercessors, nurturers, and pioneers of faith. They were not weak or secondary figures but vessels of God's mighty work on earth. From Sarah, who birthed a nation, to Mary, who bore the Savior, every woman in the Bible teaches us a unique lesson about faith, courage, and perseverance.

How Women Have Shaped History Through Faith, Courage, and Obedience

Imagine history without the boldness of Esther, the prayers of Hannah, the leadership of Deborah, or the faithfulness of Mary Magdalene. Would the nation of Israel have been preserved without Jochebed's fearless decision to hide Moses? Would the early church have thrived without Lydia's hospitality and support? The world has been profoundly shaped by women who dared to trust God, even when the odds were against them.

Consider the story of Deborah in the Old Testament. In a time when Israel was oppressed, she rose as a prophetess and judge, leading an entire nation to victory (Judges 4-5). She did not wait for a man to take action—she stepped forward in obedience to God's calling. Compare this to Priscilla in the New Testament, a woman who, alongside her husband Aquila, helped mentor Apollos, a key leader in the early church (Acts 18:24-26). These women, separated by centuries, shared the same boldness, the same obedience, and the same willingness to be used by God.

It is not just biblical history that speaks of such women—our modern world has witnessed the power of women who walk in divine purpose. From missionary pioneers like Amy Carmichael, who rescued girls from temple slavery in India, to women like Corrie ten Boom, who risked her life to save Jews during the Holocaust, history is filled with examples of women who embodied the strength, faith, and courage of biblical heroines.

The Importance of Learning from Biblical Role Models

In today's world, women face countless pressures. Society often dictates conflicting messages—telling women to be strong yet submissive, independent yet nurturing, ambitious yet self-sacrificing. Many women struggle to find their identity and purpose in the midst of these voices. This is why we must return to God's original blueprint for womanhood.

The Bible is not just a book of old stories—it is alive, relevant, and filled with lessons that apply to our daily lives. The women in Scripture were real people, with real struggles, fears, and victories. They were not perfect, yet God used them in extraordinary ways.

Take Ruth, for example. She was a foreigner, a widow, and a woman with no social status, yet God honored her faithfulness, and she became part of the lineage of Jesus (Ruth 4:13-17). In contrast, Rahab was a prostitute, yet because of her faith, she was saved and became a part of God's redemptive plan (Joshua 2, Matthew 1:5). What do these women teach us? That God does not define us by our past, but by our faith and obedience.

When we study the lives of these women, we don't just read history—we gain wisdom, encouragement, and a roadmap for our own lives. Their stories remind us that:

- ✓ Faithfulness leads to divine favor (Hannah, Mary, Ruth)

- ✓ Courage in adversity brings victory (Esther, Deborah, Rahab)
- ✓ Prayer changes destinies (Hannah, Elizabeth, the Persistent Widow)
- ✓ God uses the unexpected (Hagar, the Samaritan Woman, Priscilla)
- ✓ A life surrendered to God leaves a lasting impact (Mary, Lois & Eunice, Lydia)

Overview of the 20 Women We Will Study

This book will take you on a journey through the lives of 20 great women of the Bible—10 from the Old Testament and 10 from the New Testament—each revealing a unique pillar of womanhood. Every chapter will explore the life of one woman, the lessons we can learn from her, and how we can apply those truths today.

- ✓ From the Old Testament: Jochebed, Deborah, Ruth, Hannah, Abigail, Esther, Hagar, the Proverbs 31 Woman, Rahab, and Miriam.
- ✓ From the New Testament: Mary (Mother of Jesus), Elizabeth, Mary Magdalene, the Woman with the Issue of Blood, the Samaritan Woman, the Persistent Widow, Phoebe, Lydia, Priscilla, and Lois & Eunice.

Each chapter will be filled with Scripture, real-life applications, and encouragement to help you step into the fullness of God's design for womanhood. Whether you are a young woman seeking direction, a mother raising the next generation, a leader influencing others, or someone who feels forgotten and broken, this book will remind you that you are part of God's incredible plan.

Final Encouragement

As we embark on this journey, I encourage you to open your heart to God's voice. These are not just stories of the past—they are divine blueprints for the present and future. The same God who called Esther to save a nation, who saw Hagar in the wilderness, who empowered Mary Magdalene to be the first witness of the Resurrection—that same God is calling you today.

So, as you read, reflect, and apply these lessons, may you rise as a pillar of womanhood—strong in faith, courageous in purpose, and unwavering in obedience to God's call.

Reflection Questions

1. *How does Genesis 1:27-28 shape your understanding of womanhood?*
2. *Which biblical woman do you already relate to the most, and why?*
3. *In what areas of your life do you feel God is calling you to step out in faith, courage, or obedience?*
4. *What societal pressures or expectations have shaped your view of womanhood? How does Scripture challenge or affirm those views?*
5. *How can you use the lessons from these biblical women to impact your family, church, or community?*

Section 1:
Foundations of Womanhood
(Old Testament Women)

Jochebed – The Power of Faith-Filled Motherhood

Motherhood is one of the most powerful and sacred roles a woman can have. It is a divine calling, a holy assignment entrusted by God Himself. A mother is not just a caregiver; she is a shaper of destinies, a protector of purpose, and a nurturer of greatness.

One of the greatest examples of faith-filled motherhood in the Bible is Jochebed, the mother of Moses. She was not a queen like Esther, nor was she a prophetess like Deborah. She was an ordinary woman living in a time of extraordinary danger. Yet, because of her faith and courage, she raised a child who would change the course of history.

In this chapter, we will explore Jochebed's unwavering trust in God, her boldness in the face of impossible circumstances, and the vital role of mothers in shaping the future. We will also look at how faith-filled mothers today can raise children who will impact the world for God's glory.

A Mother's Faith in the Face of Fear

Jochebed's story begins in Exodus 2:1-10 during one of the darkest times in Israel's history. The Israelites had been living as slaves in Egypt for over 400 years, and Pharaoh, fearing their growing population, issued a brutal decree: every Hebrew baby boy must be thrown into the Nile River and killed.

Can you imagine the terror in the hearts of Hebrew mothers? To carry a child for nine months, to feel his little kicks, to dream of his future, only to know that if he were a boy, he would be taken from your arms and drowned?

Yet, in the midst of this cruelty, Jochebed refused to surrender to fear. When she gave birth to a baby boy, she saw that he was no ordinary child (Exodus 2:2). But more than his physical beauty, she recognized God's hand upon his life. Instead of giving in to hopelessness, she chose faith over fear.

For three months, she hid him, defying the king's order. Every cry, every movement was a risk, but she believed that if God had given her this child, He had a plan for him. Faith does not ignore danger, but it believes that God's purpose is greater than the threat.

When she could hide him no longer, she placed him in a basket and set him afloat on the Nile. This was not an act of abandonment, but an act of surrender. She released him into God's hands, trusting that the same river meant for destruction would become a path to deliverance.

And God honored her faith. Pharaoh's own daughter found Moses, had compassion on him, and unknowingly paid Jochebed to nurse her own son! The very system that sought to destroy Moses became the tool God used to preserve him.

This is the power of a faith-filled mother—one who does not bow to fear, but entrusts her child to the divine purpose of God.

Shaping the Destiny of a Nation

Jochebed was not just a woman of faith; she was a mother of influence. Though she had only a short time to raise Moses before he was taken to Pharaoh's palace, she laid a foundation of faith in his heart that shaped his destiny.

We don't know exactly what she taught him in those early years, but we do know that when Moses grew older, he chose to identify with the people of God rather than enjoy the sinful pleasures of Egypt (Hebrews 11:24-26). This means that the values instilled by his mother were so deeply rooted in him that even in the palace of Pharaoh, surrounded by luxury and power, he never forgot who he truly was.

This shows us an incredible truth: a mother's influence can shape a child's purpose even in the midst of a godless culture.

In today's world, Christian mothers face similar challenges. The world constantly tries to shape children's minds with false ideologies, moral compromises, and distractions that pull them away from God. But a mother who prays, teaches, and models faith can anchor her children in God's truth, no matter what environment they are placed in.

Jochebed reminds us that mothers are not just raising children—they are raising leaders, prophets, world-changers, and kingdom warriors. Even when the world is hostile to their faith, God's plan for them will not be stopped.

Real-Life Example: Mothers Who Raise World-Changers

Throughout history, we see the power of godly mothers shaping the lives of those who changed the world. One powerful example is Susanna Wesley, the mother of John and Charles Wesley.

Susanna had 19 children, and though she lived in poverty, she devoted herself to raising them in the fear of the Lord. She spent hours in prayer, and despite her difficult circumstances, she made sure her children were grounded in the Word of God.

Her son, John Wesley, went on to lead one of the greatest revivals in history, preaching to thousands and transforming England with the gospel. Charles Wesley became one of the greatest hymn writers of

all time. But behind their success was the faith and perseverance of a mother who refused to compromise on their spiritual upbringing.
Just like Jochebed, Susanna raised her children with faith, even in adversity, and through them, millions were impacted for the kingdom of God.

Encouragement for Mothers Today

Jochebed's story is a reminder that a mother's faith can change the course of history. You may not know the full impact of your prayers, your sacrifices, or your teachings, but God does.
Maybe you are raising children in a difficult environment, struggling with challenges, or wondering if your influence really matters. Do not lose heart.
The nights you spend praying over your child's future? God hears you.
The times you teach them God's Word when they would rather play? Seeds are being planted.
The moments when you feel exhausted and unnoticed? God sees you, and your work is not in vain.
Just as God honored Jochebed's faith, He will honor yours. The children you raise today can become the leaders, preachers, missionaries, and kingdom-builders of tomorrow.
Even if your child is in a "Pharaoh's palace" today—surrounded by a godless culture—remember that the foundation you lay in their early years will never be erased.

Reflection Questions

1. *Jochebed had faith in God's plan for Moses, even when circumstances seemed hopeless.*

In what areas of your life do you need to trust God with your children or future?

2. *Moses' identity was shaped by the faith his mother instilled in him. What spiritual foundations are you laying in your home?*
3. *Jochebed surrendered Moses into God's hands. Is there something in your life—your child, your plans, your future—that God is asking you to release into His hands?*
4. *Susanna Wesley raised world-changers despite poverty and hardship. How can you be more intentional in shaping the next generation for God's purposes?*
5. *What steps can you take today to deepen your own faith so you can model it for those around you?*

Final Encouragement

Jochebed's story is not just about a woman from ancient times—it is about you. The world may not know your name, but Heaven does. The children you nurture, the prayers you whisper, the faith you model—they all matter.

Like Jochebed, stand firm in faith, trust God's plan, and know that your role as a mother or spiritual mentor is one of the most powerful callings on earth. The world may see an ordinary woman, but God sees a history-maker.

Deborah – Boldness and Leadership in Action

Leadership is often associated with strength, vision, and authority, but true leadership is much more than that. It is about serving with wisdom, standing firm in faith, and inspiring others to step into their calling.
History has long been dominated by male leaders, yet God has always raised up women to fulfill significant roles in His divine plan. One such woman was Deborah, the only female judge of Israel.
In a time when Israel had fallen into spiritual and moral decay, Deborah rose as a beacon of wisdom, boldness, and spiritual authority. She was not just a judge—she was a prophetess, a military strategist, and a leader who commanded the respect of an entire nation.
This chapter will explore Deborah's incredible leadership, the lessons we can learn from her boldness, and how God continues to use women to break barriers and lead with strength today.

A Leader in a Time of Crisis

Deborah's story unfolds in Judges 4-5 during one of the most chaotic periods in Israel's history. After the death of Joshua, the Israelites fell into cycles of sin and rebellion, repeatedly turning away from God. Because of their disobedience, God allowed them to be oppressed by foreign nations as a means of calling them back to Him.
At this time, King Jabin of Canaan and his ruthless military commander, Sisera, had cruelly oppressed Israel for 20 years. Sisera's army was unbeatable, equipped with 900 iron chariots, a military force far superior to Israel's. The people were living in fear,

and no one had the courage to rise up against their oppressors.

It was in this time of national despair that Deborah emerged as Israel's leader. She was not a warrior like Joshua, nor a king like David. She was a woman called by God to lead His people.

Deborah: A Woman of Wisdom and Spiritual Authority

The Bible introduces Deborah as *"a prophetess, the wife of Lappidoth, who was judging Israel at that time"* (Judges 4:4). She did not gain her position through inheritance, political power, or military strength. Instead, she was chosen by God because of her wisdom, discernment, and faithfulness.

Unlike other judges who led through brute force, Deborah led through wisdom and spiritual insight. The people of Israel would come to her, seeking counsel and justice. She was not just a leader—she was a voice of God to the nation.

Her leadership teaches us that true authority does not come from position or power, but from God's anointing. Leadership is not about titles—it is about influence, wisdom, and obedience to God's calling.

The Call to Battle: Courage in Action

One of the greatest marks of Deborah's leadership was her willingness to act with boldness when others were afraid.

In Judges 4:6-7, Deborah sent for Barak, a military commander, and gave him a divine message:

"The Lord, the God of Israel, commands you: 'Go, take with you ten thousand men… and lead them up to Mount Tabor. I will lure Sisera… and give him into your hands.'"

This was not just a military strategy—it was a prophetic word from God.

However, Barak hesitated. He was afraid to go into battle without Deborah by his side. His response in Judges 4:8 was telling:

"If you go with me, I will go; but if you don't go with me, I won't go."

Barak's hesitation revealed a lack of faith, but Deborah did not back down. She courageously agreed to go, but she made it clear that because of Barak's reluctance, the honor of the victory would go to a woman, not to him.

This was a shocking declaration in a male-dominated society, but it was a reminder that God uses whomever He chooses, regardless of gender, background, or status.

With Deborah's encouragement, Barak led the army of Israel into battle—and God gave them victory. The mighty army of Sisera was thrown into chaos, and their iron chariots became useless in the mud as the Lord caused a supernatural storm. Sisera fled on foot, only to be killed by another woman—Jael, who drove a tent peg through his head (Judges 4:21).

A Song of Victory: Celebrating God's Deliverance

After the battle, Deborah and Barak sang a song of triumph in Judges 5. This was no ordinary song—it was a declaration of God's faithfulness and a reminder of how He uses ordinary people to accomplish His will.

One of the most powerful lines in this song is Judges 5:7:

"Villagers in Israel would not fight; they held back until I, Deborah, arose, until I arose, a mother in Israel."

This verse reveals something beautiful about Deborah's heart. She did not see herself as a queen, a warrior, or a ruler—she saw herself as a mother to the nation.

This is the essence of godly leadership—leading with the heart of a parent, protecting, guiding, and nurturing those under your care.

Deborah's song is a reminder that when God raises up a leader, it is not for personal glory, but for His divine purpose.

Breaking Barriers: Women in Leadership Today

Deborah's story is not just about one woman in ancient Israel—it is about every woman who has ever been called to lead in a world that doubts her.

Throughout history, women have faced opposition, yet God has continued to raise them up in business, ministry, politics, and beyond.

One powerful modern example is Corrie ten Boom. During World War II, she and her family risked their lives to hide Jews from the Nazis. When she was eventually arrested and sent to a concentration camp, she continued to minister to those around her. After surviving the war, she traveled the world, preaching about forgiveness, faith, and the power of God.

Like Deborah, Corrie was a woman of wisdom, courage, and unwavering faith. She stood firm when others faltered, led when others feared, and trusted God even in the face of death.

Deborah's story reminds us that when God calls a woman to lead, He equips her with everything she needs. Whether in a boardroom, a church, a home, or a battlefield, God's anointing is not bound by gender—it is bound by faithfulness.

Reflection Questions

1. *Deborah led with wisdom and faith in a time of crisis. How can you develop spiritual discernment and boldness in your own leadership?*
2. *Barak hesitated when God called him to battle. Are there areas in your life where you are delaying obedience due to fear?*
3. *Deborah saw herself as "a mother in Israel." How can you lead with a nurturing, servant-hearted spirit in your family, workplace, or community?*
4. *God used two women—Deborah and Jael—to defeat Israel's enemy. How does this challenge traditional ideas about leadership and courage?*
5. *What are some ways you can encourage and support women in leadership today?*

Final Encouragement

Deborah's story is a powerful testimony that God calls and equips those who are willing to trust Him. It doesn't matter whether you are male or female, young or old, rich or poor—if God has called you, He will go before you.

Like Deborah, may you rise boldly, lead courageously, and trust fully in God's power to work through you.

The world may doubt you, but if God is for you, who can stand against you?

Ruth – Loyalty and Redemption

Life is full of unexpected twists and turns. There are moments of joy and moments of deep sorrow. But within every hardship lies an opportunity for God to reveal His grace, favor, and redemptive power.

The story of Ruth is one of the most profound examples of loyalty, faithfulness, and divine redemption in the Bible. A Moabite woman who had every reason to walk away from her past instead chose to stay, and because of her unwavering commitment, God orchestrated a beautiful new beginning.

This chapter will take you on a journey through Ruth's life, showing how faithfulness leads to favor and how God restores and rebuilds even the most broken situations.

A Decision of Unshakable Loyalty

The story of Ruth begins in a time of deep famine and loss.

A man named Elimelech and his wife Naomi, along with their two sons, left Bethlehem in search of food and settled in the land of Moab (Ruth 1:1-2). Moab was an enemy nation to Israel, known for its idolatry and opposition to God's people. Yet, out of desperation, they moved there to survive.

While in Moab, Naomi's two sons married Moabite women—Orpah and Ruth.

But tragedy struck. First, Elimelech died. Then, Naomi's two sons also passed away, leaving her and her daughters-in-law as widows with no protection, no provision, and no future (Ruth 1:3-5).

In ancient times, widowhood was one of the most vulnerable positions a woman could be in. There were no jobs or social security for widows. Without a husband or male relative, a woman had little hope of survival.

Naomi, brokenhearted and bitter, decided to return to her homeland in Bethlehem, where she had heard that God had restored the land with food (Ruth 1:6). Knowing that she had nothing left to offer, she urged her daughters-in-law to return to their own families and find new husbands.

At first, both Orpah and Ruth wept and refused to leave Naomi's side. But when Naomi insisted, Orpah eventually kissed her goodbye and left.

But Ruth… Ruth clung to Naomi.

Her response is one of the most beautiful declarations of loyalty ever spoken (Ruth 1:16-17):

"Don't urge me to leave you or to turn back from you. Where you go, I will go, and where you stay, I will stay. Your people will be my people and your God my God. Where you die, I will die, and there I will be buried. May the Lord deal with me, be it ever so severely, if even death separates you and me."

This was not just a statement of devotion to Naomi—it was a powerful commitment to the God of Israel.

As a Moabite, Ruth had grown up in a pagan land, worshipping false gods. But through Naomi, she had come to know the One True God. Her decision to stay was not just about loyalty to her mother-in-law—it was about choosing to walk in faith with God, no matter the cost.

Faithfulness Leads to Favor

When Naomi and Ruth arrived in Bethlehem, they were still poor, widowed, and uncertain of what the future held.

In Israelite culture, widows had the right to glean in the fields—meaning they could pick up leftover grain

that the harvesters had missed. It was a provision for the poor, but it was also humbling, hard labor.
Ruth, however, did not hesitate to work diligently to provide for Naomi. She stepped out in faith and went into the fields to glean, not knowing that her faithfulness would position her for divine favor.
It was in those very fields that she caught the attention of Boaz, a wealthy landowner and a relative of Naomi's late husband.
Boaz noticed Ruth's humility, hard work, and unwavering commitment to Naomi. He blessed her, saying:
"May the Lord repay you for what you have done. May you be richly rewarded by the Lord, the God of Israel, under whose wings you have come to take refuge." (Ruth 2:12)
Ruth's simple act of faithfulness—showing up to the fields and working hard—opened the door for God's abundant provision.

Redemption: A New Beginning

As a close relative of Naomi's family, Boaz was in a position to be a "kinsman-redeemer." In Israelite custom, a kinsman-redeemer was a male relative who could marry a widow and restore the family's inheritance.
Naomi, realizing that Boaz was a godly man and had shown kindness to Ruth, instructed her to go to him and make a request for redemption.
In an act of humility and trust, Ruth approached Boaz at night and lay at his feet, a symbolic gesture of submission. She asked him to spread the corner of his garment over her (Ruth 3:9), a request that signified marriage and protection.
Boaz was deeply moved by her character and faith, and he responded:

"The Lord bless you, my daughter. This kindness is greater than that which you showed earlier... I will do for you all you ask." (Ruth 3:10-11)

Boaz took the necessary steps to redeem Ruth, and soon, they were married.

Ruth, the widowed foreigner, once poor and destitute, was now the wife of a wealthy, godly man.

Her loyalty had led to redemption.

Her faithfulness had led to divine favor.

And the most astonishing part?

Ruth became the great-grandmother of King David (Ruth 4:17) and is one of only five women mentioned in the genealogy of Jesus Christ (Matthew 1:5).

A Moabite woman, once an outsider, became a key part of God's plan of redemption for the world.

New Testament Reflection: The Ultimate Redeemer

Ruth's story is a powerful foreshadowing of Jesus Christ.

Just as Boaz redeemed Ruth, Jesus is our Kinsman-Redeemer.

We were once outsiders, lost in sin, much like Ruth in Moab.

We had no hope, just as she had nothing to offer Naomi.

But because of His great love, Jesus came to redeem us, just as Boaz did for Ruth.

Titus 2:14 says:

"[Jesus] gave himself for us to redeem us from all wickedness and to purify for himself a people that are his very own, eager to do what is good."

Just as Ruth found favor and security under Boaz's covering, we find eternal security under the covering of Christ.

Reflection Questions

1. *Ruth remained loyal to Naomi even when she had no guarantee of a better future. Is there an area in your life where God is calling you to remain faithful, even when the outcome is uncertain?*
2. *Boaz noticed Ruth's character before anything else. What qualities of faithfulness and integrity are you cultivating in your daily life?*
3. *Ruth's redemption story foreshadows Jesus' redemption for us. How does understanding Christ as your Redeemer change the way you view your relationship with Him?*
4. *Are there people in your life who need encouragement and support, just as Ruth supported Naomi? How can you extend loyalty and kindness to those around you?*
5. *If God could take a foreigner, a widow, and an outcast like Ruth and use her in His grand plan, what does that say about how He can use you?*

Final Encouragement

Ruth's story is proof that faithfulness leads to favor, and loyalty leads to legacy.

No matter where you come from, God can write a new story for your life.

He is still in the business of redeeming brokenness and turning sorrow into joy.

Like Ruth, may you walk forward in faith, knowing that your Redeemer lives.

Hannah – The Strength of a Praying Woman

There are moments in life when our deepest desires seem completely out of reach. We pray, we hope, we cry out to God, and yet the heavens seem silent. The weight of waiting, especially when the longing is deep, can be unbearable. But there is something powerful about a woman who refuses to give up, a woman who takes her pain to God in prayer and refuses to let go until she sees His hand move.

Hannah's story is one of heartache, perseverance, and divine intervention. She was a woman who knew what it meant to suffer in silence, to be misunderstood, and to feel forgotten. But her story didn't end there—her story is a testimony of what happens when a woman prays with unwavering faith and trusts God's perfect timing.

This chapter will walk through Hannah's journey, the power of persistent prayer, and the legacy that comes from dedicating what we receive back to God.

A Heartbreaking Delay

Hannah's story begins in 1 Samuel 1, during a time in Israel's history when having children was considered a woman's highest honor. It wasn't just about personal fulfillment—it was about carrying on a family's name, securing an inheritance, and fulfilling God's command to be fruitful and multiply.

But Hannah had a problem that seemed impossible to fix—she was barren.

Her husband, Elkanah, loved her deeply, but he had another wife, Peninnah, who was able to have children. And Peninnah, instead of showing compassion, constantly mocked and tormented Hannah for her infertility (1 Samuel 1:6).

Every year, Elkanah would take his family to Shiloh to worship and offer sacrifices to the Lord. And every year, Hannah would be reminded of what she lacked. Peninnah would provoke her, and the pain would overwhelm her.

One year, it became too much to bear. Hannah was so distressed that she could not even eat. Instead of lashing out at Peninnah or taking her frustration out on Elkanah, she took her pain to God.

She went to the tabernacle in Shiloh, knelt before the Lord, and wept bitterly.

And in her brokenness, she made a vow that would change everything:

"Lord Almighty, if You will only look on Your servant's misery and remember me, and not forget Your servant but give her a son, then I will give him to the Lord for all the days of his life." (1 Samuel 1:11)

Hannah did something remarkable—she did not just ask for a child for herself, but she surrendered him to God even before he was conceived.

This was no ordinary request. She wasn't bargaining with God or trying to manipulate Him. She was saying, **"Lord, if You bless me, I will not hold onto the blessing for myself. I will give it back to You."**

This kind of surrender moves the heart of God.

The Power of Persistent Prayer

As Hannah was praying, the priest Eli saw her. Her lips were moving, but no sound came out. Eli misunderstood her agony and assumed she was drunk (1 Samuel 1:13-14).

Think about that for a moment—Hannah was pouring out her soul, praying with everything inside of her, and yet even the priest did not recognize her faith.

How often do we feel like no one understands our prayers? How often do we cry out to God, only to be met with silence from heaven and misunderstanding from people?

But Hannah was not deterred. She explained her sorrow to Eli, and instead of defending herself, she simply said:

"I am a woman who is deeply troubled… I was pouring out my soul to the Lord." (1 Samuel 1:15)

Eli, seeing her sincerity, spoke a blessing over her:

"*Go in peace, and may the God of Israel grant you what you have asked of Him."* (1 Samuel 1:17)

And here is the beautiful part—Hannah left with a heart full of peace, even before her circumstances changed.

She was no longer downcast because she had placed her request in the hands of the One who could answer it.

And in God's perfect timing, Hannah conceived and gave birth to a son—Samuel.

Dedicating the Blessing Back to God

When Samuel was born, Hannah could have easily held onto him tightly. She had waited so long, endured so much, and now she had finally received what she prayed for.

But she remembered her vow.

When Samuel was weaned, she brought him to the house of the Lord at Shiloh and told Eli:

"I prayed for this child, and the Lord has granted me what I asked of Him. So now I give him to the Lord. For his whole life, he will be given over to the Lord." (1 Samuel 1:27-28)

She left her miracle child in the temple, under the care of Eli, to serve the Lord.

And because of Hannah's faithfulness, Samuel became one of the greatest prophets in Israel's history.
He was the one who anointed King David. He was the one who stood as a voice for God in a time of spiritual decline.
And it all started because one woman prayed, trusted, and surrendered.
New Testament Reflection: A Mother's Influence
Hannah's story reminds us of another mother who dedicated her son to God—Mary, the mother of Jesus.
When the angel Gabriel told Mary that she would bear the Son of God, she responded with the same attitude of surrender as Hannah:
"I am the Lord's servant… May Your word to me be fulfilled." (Luke 1:38)
Just as Hannah gave up Samuel for God's purpose, Mary would one day watch her Son give His life for the salvation of the world.
Hannah's prayer brought forth a prophet.
Mary's obedience brought forth the Messiah.
Both stories show us that when we dedicate what we love to God, He does far greater things than we can imagine.
Modern Mothers Who Birth Spiritual Movements
Throughout history, many mothers of faith have followed Hannah's example and raised world-changers through prayer.
Susanna Wesley, the mother of John and Charles Wesley, spent hours in prayer for her children. Her dedication led to the birth of the Methodist movement.
Monica, the mother of St. Augustine, prayed fervently for her rebellious son. Her prayers led him to

salvation, and he became one of the greatest theologians in church history.

A praying woman does not just impact her own life—she changes generations.

Reflection Questions

1. *Hannah did not give up when her prayers seemed unanswered. Are there areas in your life where God is calling you to remain persistent in prayer?*
2. *Hannah surrendered Samuel before he was even born. Is there something in your life that you need to dedicate back to God?*
3. *Hannah left the temple with peace even before she saw her answer. How can you cultivate that same trust in God's timing?*
4. *Think about the legacy you are building. What spiritual seeds are you planting today that could impact future generations?*

Final Encouragement

Hannah's story teaches us that prayer is not just about getting what we want—it's about surrendering to God's will.

A woman who prays can move heaven, shift circumstances, and birth destinies.

May you be that woman. May you trust, pray, and surrender—knowing that God hears, God remembers, and God answers in His perfect time.

Abigail – Wisdom That Prevents Disaster

There are moments in life when disaster is just around the corner, when emotions run high, tempers flare, and one wrong decision could lead to irreversible consequences. It is in these moments that wisdom—true, God-given wisdom—becomes the difference between ruin and redemption.

Abigail was a woman who understood the power of wisdom, discretion, and quick thinking. Her story is one of courage, humility, and intelligence. She was a woman who stood between wrath and destruction and turned away disaster with nothing but the force of her words and her wisdom.

Her life teaches us that a single wise person can prevent destruction, restore peace, and change the course of history.

A Fool's Folly and a Woman's Wisdom

The story of Abigail is found in 1 Samuel 25, in the days when David was fleeing from King Saul. David and his men had been living in the wilderness, trying to survive as outlaws, even though David had done nothing wrong.

At this time, there was a wealthy man named Nabal who owned vast flocks of sheep and goats. He was an influential landowner, but his greatest weakness was his foolishness and arrogance. His name, Nabal, literally means *"fool,"* and his actions reflected the meaning of his name.

David's men had been protecting Nabal's shepherds in the wilderness. They had guarded his flocks, ensured that no harm came to his workers, and treated them with respect. When the time of feasting came, David sent messengers to Nabal, humbly asking for provisions. It was a reasonable request—David had shown kindness to Nabal, and now, in his time of need, he was simply asking for kindness in return.

But Nabal responded with insults and mockery.

"Who is this David? Who is this son of Jesse? Many servants are running away from their masters these days." (1 Samuel 25:10)

His words were dripping with contempt. Instead of showing gratitude, he treated David like a nobody, dismissing him as if he were worthless.

When David's men returned and told him what Nabal had said, David was furious.

He strapped on his sword and commanded his men to do the same. *"May God deal with me severely if by morning I leave alive one male of all who belong to Nabal."* (1 Samuel 25:22)

David—a man after God's own heart—was about to commit a massacre. His rage had clouded his judgment, and he was ready to take justice into his own hands.

This was a crisis moment. A wise person was needed to prevent disaster.

And that wise person was Abigail.

A Woman of Wisdom and Action

Abigail was Nabal's wife, but she was nothing like him. Where he was foolish, she was discerning. Where he was arrogant, she was humble. Where he was reckless, she was wise.

When one of Nabal's servants heard how Nabal had insulted David, he rushed to Abigail and told her what had happened.

The servant knew that disaster was coming. *"Disaster is hanging over our master and his whole household," he said. "He is such a wicked man that no one can talk to him."* (1 Samuel 25:17)

Abigail did not waste time. She didn't panic. She didn't argue with Nabal. She took immediate action.

She quickly gathered supplies—200 loaves of bread, two skins of wine, five dressed sheep, roasted grain, cakes of figs, and raisins—and set out to meet David before he could reach Nabal's household.

As she rode out, she saw David and his men approaching, swords in hand, anger burning in their eyes.

And in that moment, Abigail did something incredible. Instead of waiting for David to attack, she got off her donkey and bowed before him.

She took responsibility for the situation, even though she was not the one who had done wrong. She humbled herself and spoke words of wisdom that diffused David's anger and changed the entire course of events.

"My lord, let the blame be on me alone… Please pay no attention to that wicked man Nabal. He is just like his name—his name means Fool, and folly goes with him." (1 Samuel 25:24-25)

She reminded David of who he truly was.

She reminded him that he was called to a higher purpose and that taking revenge with his own hands would only lead to regret.

"The Lord your God will certainly make a lasting dynasty for my master, because he fights the Lord's battles. Let no wrongdoing be found in you as long as you live." (1 Samuel 25:28)

She spoke to his destiny, not his anger.

She reminded him that God was in control and that shedding innocent blood would only bring guilt upon him.

And David—who had been ready to kill every man in Nabal's household—stopped.

Her wisdom saved lives.

David recognized that Abigail was God's instrument to prevent him from making a terrible mistake.

"Praise be to the Lord, the God of Israel, who has sent you today to meet me. May you be blessed for your good judgment and for keeping me from bloodshed this day." (1 Samuel 25:32-33)

Disaster had been averted—because one woman had the courage to speak wisely and act quickly.

The Power of Peacemakers in Conflict-Ridden Homes and Workplaces

Abigail's story is not just about one woman in ancient Israel. It is about the power of wisdom and discretion in every area of life.

How many conflicts in homes, marriages, workplaces, and churches could be avoided if someone was willing to step in with wisdom and humility?

In a marriage, a wise spouse can prevent years of resentment with a single moment of humility and grace.

In a workplace, a wise leader can diffuse tension before it turns into a toxic environment.

In a family, a wise parent can break cycles of anger and division by choosing wisdom over retaliation.

In the New Testament, Jesus taught the same principle:

"Blessed are the peacemakers, for they will be called children of God." (Matthew 5:9)

Peacemakers are not passive. They act boldly, like Abigail. They step into difficult situations and speak words of wisdom that prevent destruction.

Reflection Questions

1. *Have you ever been in a situation where conflict was about to escalate? How did you respond?*
2. *What can you learn from Abigail's wisdom and quick action?*
3. *Are there areas in your life—family, work, friendships—where God is calling you to be a peacemaker?*
4. *How can you practice humility and wisdom in your interactions with others, even when you are not at fault?*

Final Encouragement

Abigail's story teaches us that wisdom is more powerful than anger, and humility is more effective than pride.

You don't have to be the strongest person in the room. You don't have to be the loudest voice in the argument.

You just need wisdom.

And wisdom—God's wisdom—can save lives, restore peace, and change destinies.

Esther – Courage to Stand for God's People

Some moments in life define everything. They come as unexpected crossroads, demanding a choice—one that could change the future forever. These moments are terrifying, but they are also the moments where faith, courage, and destiny collide.

For Queen Esther, such a moment came when she had to decide whether she would risk everything—her position, her comfort, even her life—to stand up for the people of God.

She was a woman of divine purpose, placed in the palace not for luxury, but for a mission. And though fear threatened to hold her back, she chose faith over fear and courage over comfort.

Her story is not just one of royalty—it is one of bravery, divine positioning, and the power of preparation and prayer.

A Hidden Queen in a Foreign Land

The book of Esther unfolds during a time when the Jewish people were living under Persian rule. The great empire of Persia, ruled by King Xerxes (also called Ahasuerus), stretched across 127 provinces, and in the heart of it stood the magnificent palace of Susa.

The story begins with an unexpected vacancy in the palace—Queen Vashti had been removed from her position because she refused to obey the king. To find a new queen, Xerxes held a royal beauty contest, gathering the most beautiful young women in the empire.

Among them was Esther, a Jewish orphan raised by her cousin Mordecai. She was a young woman of grace, intelligence, and quiet strength. Though she was a Jew, she was advised to keep her identity a secret for the time being.

God's hand was on Esther. Out of all the women brought to the palace, the king was drawn to her, and she was crowned queen.

At first, it seemed like Esther's new life would be one of ease. But God had placed her there for more than just beauty and comfort—He had placed her there for a purpose.

A Deadly Decree and a Moment of Decision

Unbeknownst to Esther, a storm was brewing against her people.

A man named Haman, a high-ranking official in the Persian empire, had a deep hatred for the Jews. He was enraged when Mordecai, Esther's cousin, refused to bow to him. His pride was so wounded that he didn't just want revenge against Mordecai—he wanted to wipe out the entire Jewish people.

Haman tricked King Xerxes into signing a decree ordering the destruction of all Jews in the Persian Empire.

It was an irrevocable law—on a certain date, every Jew, young and old, man and woman, would be slaughtered.

Panic spread. The Jewish people began mourning, fasting, and crying out to God.

Mordecai sent word to Esther, urging her to go before the king and plead for the lives of her people.

But this was no simple request.

There was a strict law in Persia—no one, not even the queen, could approach the king uninvited. The punishment? Death.

Esther knew that if she went to the king without being summoned, she could be executed on the spot.

She hesitated. Fear gripped her heart.

And that's when Mordecai sent the most famous words in the book of Esther—words that still ring true today:

"Who knows whether you have come to the kingdom for such a time as this?" (Esther 4:14)

It was a call to courage. A call to step into the destiny God had prepared for her.

And in that moment, Esther made a choice.

She cast off her fear and embraced her divine assignment.

"I will go to the king, even though it is against the law. And if I perish, I perish." (Esther 4:16)

She risked everything—because some things are worth dying for.

The Power of Preparation, Strategy, and Prayer

Esther didn't rush into the king's presence impulsively. She understood the power of preparation.

Before she took action, she called for a three-day fast.

She prayed. She sought God. She aligned herself with divine wisdom.

Then, instead of storming into the throne room with desperate pleas, she approached the situation with strategy.

She invited the king and Haman to a banquet—not once, but twice. She created an atmosphere where the king was receptive, where Haman was unsuspecting, and where her request would be met with favor.

Timing mattered. Wisdom mattered. Discernment mattered.

And when the moment finally came, Esther revealed the truth—that Haman had orchestrated a plan to annihilate her people.

The king was outraged. Haman was exposed. And the very gallows that Haman had built to execute Mordecai? He was hanged on them himself.

The Jewish people were saved—because one woman had the courage to stand.

Women Who Stand for Justice Today

Esther's story is not just an ancient tale—it is a blueprint for bold women today.

Across the world, there are women who, like Esther, are stepping up to fight for justice, even at great personal risk.

Women who fight against human trafficking, risking their lives to rescue the oppressed.

Women who stand for the unborn, defending the voiceless.

Women who speak out against corruption, exposing evil in high places.

Like Esther, they count the cost and stand anyway.

In the New Testament, Jesus honored bold women who took a stand—like the persistent widow who kept pleading for justice (Luke 18:1-8), or the woman who broke all cultural barriers to anoint His feet (Luke 7:37-38).

Courage is costly—but the reward is great.

Reflection Questions

1. *What fears hold you back from stepping into God's calling for your life?*
2. *Have you ever found yourself in a position where speaking up felt dangerous? How did you respond?*

3. *Are there areas in your life where God is calling you to be bold like Esther?*
4. *How can you prepare spiritually—through prayer and fasting—before making big decisions?*

Final Encouragement

Esther's story is a reminder that God places people in positions for divine purposes.

You are not where you are by accident.

Your job, your community, your sphere of influence—it's not just random.

God has placed you there for such a time as this.

The question is: Will you have the courage to stand?

Hagar – Finding God in the Wilderness

Some stories in the Bible feel distant, almost too grand to be relatable. But then there are stories like Hagar's—raw, painful, and deeply human. Hers is a story of rejection, loneliness, and survival. But it is also a story of divine encounter, where the God of the universe stops everything to see a woman who felt unseen, unloved, and discarded.

If you have ever felt abandoned, mistreated, or struggled in the wilderness of life, then Hagar's story is for you.

She reminds us that even when the world pushes you away, God sees you. He hears your cries. And He provides—right in the middle of the wilderness.

A Woman Caught in Someone Else's Story

Hagar was never supposed to be the main character. At least, that's how people saw her.

She was an Egyptian servant, a woman without much say in her own life. She belonged to Sarah, the wife of Abraham, and was caught up in their story—a story of waiting, impatience, and ultimately, heartbreak.

God had promised Abraham and Sarah a son, an heir who would bring forth a great nation. But as years passed and no child came, Sarah decided to take matters into her own hands. She gave Hagar to Abraham as a surrogate, hoping that through her, she would build a family (Genesis 16:1-2).

Hagar became pregnant, and for the first time in her life, she had something that Sarah did not. And that changed everything.

Sarah grew jealous, and tensions between them exploded. Sarah mistreated Hagar so harshly that she ran away into the wilderness.

Can you imagine what that felt like?

Hagar had done nothing wrong, yet she found herself alone in the desert—pregnant, abandoned, and with nowhere to go.

That's when God showed up.

Encountering God in the Wilderness

As Hagar sat by a spring of water in the desert, something happened that changed her life forever.

An angel of the Lord appeared to her.

This was not just any angelic encounter—this was the first recorded instance in Scripture where God personally sought out a woman.

And what did God say?

Did He scold her for running away? Did He dismiss her pain? No.

He asked her a question:

"Hagar, servant of Sarai, where have you come from, and where are you going?" (Genesis 16:8)

This was not a question for information—God already knew the answers. This was a question meant to reach into the depths of her heart.

And in that moment, God did something extraordinary.

He called her by name.

The world saw Hagar as a servant, but God saw her as a person.

He then made a promise:

"I will increase your descendants so much that they will be too numerous to count." (Genesis 16:10)

This was a blessing of legacy, a future for the son she carried. She was not forgotten.

Overwhelmed by this encounter, Hagar gave God a name—the only woman in the Bible to do so.
She called Him *'El Roi'*—The God Who Sees Me. (Genesis 16:13)
For the first time in her life, she knew that she was not invisible.
She returned to Abraham and Sarah, not because she was forced to, but because she now had the assurance that God was with her.

The Pain of Rejection—Again

Years passed. Hagar's son, Ishmael, grew up in Abraham's household. But then, the miracle finally happened—Sarah gave birth to Isaac, the son of promise.
At first, everything seemed fine. But tensions rose again when Sarah saw Ishmael playing with Isaac (Genesis 21:9). Sarah demanded that Hagar and Ishmael be cast out for good.
And to Abraham's heartbreak, God told him to let them go.
So, Hagar found herself in the wilderness again.
But this time, it was worse.
She wandered aimlessly with her son, watching their water run out, their strength fading, their hope slipping away.
In despair, she placed Ishmael under a bush and walked away so she wouldn't have to watch him die.
She wept bitterly.
And God heard her cries.

God's Provision in the Desert

Once again, God met Hagar in her lowest moment.
An angel called out to her:
"Do not be afraid; God has heard the boy crying as he lies there." (Genesis 21:17)

Then, God opened her eyes, and she saw a well of water.

What changed?

The well was already there. But Hagar could not see it until God opened her eyes.

And isn't that just like life?

God's provision is always near, but sometimes, we can't see it through our pain.

Hagar and Ishmael survived, and Ishmael went on to become the father of a great nation.

Her story did not end in the wilderness.

Jesus: The God Who Sees Us in Our Pain

Hagar's story is echoed in the New Testament in the way Jesus saw the unseen.

He saw the Samaritan woman at the well, giving her living water when no one else would acknowledge her (John 4:7-26).

He saw the woman caught in adultery, protecting her from condemnation (John 8:3-11).

He saw the widow at Nain, stopping a funeral just to bring her son back to life (Luke 7:11-15).

Jesus is the God who sees.

And just as He saw Hagar in the wilderness, He sees you.

Hagar's Story Today: Women Who Feel Forgotten

Hagar's story is alive in the women around us today:

The single mother, working two jobs, feeling abandoned and unseen.

The rejected woman, left alone after a painful divorce.

The girl from a broken home, searching for a place where she belongs.

To every woman who feels discarded, forgotten, or struggling to survive—Hagar's story is your story.

And God is still El Roi—The God Who Sees You.

Reflection Questions

1. *Have you ever felt invisible or forgotten? How does knowing that God sees you change that?*
2. *Are you in a wilderness season right now? What wells of provision might God be opening your eyes to?*
3. *How can Hagar's story give you hope in your own struggles?*
4. *Who in your life needs to be reminded that God sees and cares for them?*

Final Encouragement

You may feel like you're wandering through a desert.
You may feel cast out, rejected, and alone.
But God sees you.
He hears your cries.
And even when you don't see a way forward, He is already providing for you.
Your story is not over.
The God of Hagar is your God too.

The Proverbs 31 Woman – A Model of Excellence

If there is one passage in the Bible that has stirred admiration, aspiration, and even a little intimidation among women, it is Proverbs 31:10-31.

This remarkable passage describes a woman of strength, dignity, and wisdom—one who balances her faith, family, and work with grace and excellence. She is a wife, a mother, a businesswoman, a philanthropist, and a pillar of strength to those around her. She is not just a woman of beauty, but of substance, diligence, and divine purpose.

For centuries, many women have read this passage and wondered, *"Can I ever measure up?"* But the truth is, the Proverbs 31 woman is not an unreachable ideal—she is a model of what God can shape in any woman who seeks to live by His wisdom and strength.

This chapter is not about perfection—it's about pursuing excellence in every area of life while leaning on God.

A Woman of Strength and Dignity

The passage begins with a profound statement:

"A wife of noble character who can find? She is worth far more than rubies." (Proverbs 31:10)

Right away, we see that her value is rare and priceless. Her worth is not in her outward beauty, wealth, or accomplishments, but in her character—her noble heart and unwavering faith.

In the Hebrew text, the phrase "wife of noble character" is *"eshet chayil,"* which means a woman of valor, strength, and courage. This same word is used to describe warriors in battle.

This is no weak, passive woman.
She is strong, fearless, and capable.
She does not cower in the face of challenges. Instead, she rises with confidence, trusting in God's wisdom as she moves through her daily responsibilities.
In the Old Testament, we see an example of such a woman in Deborah, the judge and prophetess (Judges 4-5). She was both a spiritual leader and a military strategist, leading Israel to victory against their enemies.
Like the Proverbs 31 woman, Deborah balanced wisdom, leadership, and faithfulness to God.

The Balance of Faith, Family, and Enterprise

One of the most striking things about the Proverbs 31 woman is her ability to balance multiple roles.
She is not just a homemaker—she is a businesswoman, a provider, and a woman of great influence.
"She considers a field and buys it; out of her earnings she plants a vineyard." (Proverbs 31:16)
This verse tells us that she is financially wise and enterprising. She invests, plans, and grows her resources. She is not afraid to make decisions that will benefit her family and community.
Some might think that a godly woman is only meant to stay at home, but this passage shows otherwise. She works diligently, whether inside or outside the home.
Even in the New Testament, we see Lydia, the seller of purple cloth (Acts 16:14-15). She was a successful businesswoman, yet her heart was open to God. When she encountered Paul's preaching, she immediately embraced the gospel and used her home as a place of ministry.

Both the Proverbs 31 woman and Lydia show us that faith and enterprise are not separate—they can work together for God's glory.

A Heart of Kindness and Generosity

Beyond her diligence, the Proverbs 31 woman is known for her kindness and generosity.

"She opens her arms to the poor and extends her hands to the needy." (Proverbs 31:20)

She is not so consumed with her own success that she forgets the people around her. Instead, she gives freely, helping those in need.

We see this same heart in Tabitha (also known as Dorcas) in the New Testament (Acts 9:36-42).

Tabitha was known for her acts of charity, making clothes for widows and the poor. When she died, the community was heartbroken. But Peter, moved by the testimonies of those she had helped, prayed for her, and she was brought back to life.

What a powerful example of how a life of generosity can leave a lasting impact!

Wisdom and Influence in the Home

One of the most profound qualities of the Proverbs 31 woman is her ability to lead with wisdom and influence her household.

"She speaks with wisdom, and faithful instruction is on her tongue." (Proverbs 31:26)

She does not waste her words—her speech is filled with encouragement, truth, and grace.

In the New Testament, we see a beautiful example of this in Lois and Eunice, the grandmother and mother of Timothy (2 Timothy 1:5). Their faith shaped young Timothy into one of the key leaders in the early church.

This shows that a woman's influence goes beyond her lifetime. The way she teaches, speaks, and encourages can shape future generations.

The Secret to Her Strength

What makes the Proverbs 31 woman so remarkable? Her secret is found in the final verses:

"Charm is deceptive, and beauty is fleeting; but a woman who fears the LORD is to be praised." (Proverbs 31:30)

Her fear of the Lord—her deep respect, love, and obedience to God—is what sets her apart.

She does not rely on external beauty or worldly success to define her. Instead, her foundation is her relationship with God.

This is the key to true excellence.

The Proverbs 31 Woman Today

The Proverbs 31 woman is not just an ancient model—she exists today.

She is:

- ✓ The working mother who rises early to care for her children while excelling in her career.
- ✓ The entrepreneur who builds a business with integrity and faith.
- ✓ The ministry leader who pours wisdom into the lives of those around her.
- ✓ The single woman who uses her gifts and talents to serve God with diligence.
- ✓ She is every woman who chooses to live with faith, purpose, and excellence.

Reflection Questions

1. *What part of the Proverbs 31 woman's character do you relate to the most?*

2. *In what areas of your life do you feel God is calling you to greater diligence and excellence?*
3. *How can you balance faith, family, and enterprise in a way that honors God?*
4. *Who are the women in your life that inspire you to pursue wisdom and virtue?*
5. *What practical steps can you take to become a woman of strength, generosity, and influence?*

Final Encouragement

The Proverbs 31 woman is not a standard of perfection but a picture of what God can do in any woman who walks with Him.

She is not born this way—she becomes this woman through faith, wisdom, and a heart fully surrendered to God.

You don't have to do everything at once.

Start where you are.

Pursue God.

Work diligently.

Speak with wisdom.

And trust that, in time, God will shape you into a woman of excellence—a woman who is truly "worth more than rubies."

Rahab – A Past Doesn't Define Your Future

Some stories in the Bible remind us that God does not see people the way the world does. Society may look at someone and label them by their past—their failures, mistakes, and sins—but God sees who they can become through faith.

One of the most powerful examples of this truth is Rahab, a woman whose past should have disqualified her but whose faith made her one of the most remarkable figures in biblical history.

Rahab was a prostitute in Jericho, living on the outskirts of society, likely looked down upon by her own people. Yet, despite her past, she became a woman honored by God, saved by grace, and written into the very genealogy of Jesus Christ.

Her story is a message of hope, redemption, and the power of transformation. No matter what mistakes a person has made, no matter how broken their past may seem, God's grace is greater.

Rahab's Story – A Woman with a Scandalous Past

Rahab first appears in the Bible in Joshua 2, during a time when the Israelites, under the leadership of Joshua, were preparing to conquer the city of Jericho.

Jericho was a fortified city, well-protected by strong walls and an army that believed they were invincible. But the people of Jericho had heard the stories of Israel's God—the God who had parted the Red Sea, defeated mighty kings, and led His people with power.

Rahab, like everyone else in the city, had heard these stories. But unlike the others, she believed.

When two Israelite spies entered Jericho to assess the land, they found shelter in Rahab's house. It was a strategic hiding place—her home was built into the city wall, an easy place for travelers to stay. The king of Jericho soon heard that spies had entered the city and ordered Rahab to hand them over.

But Rahab made a bold decision: she hid the spies.

She risked everything—her safety, her life, her future—because she believed that Israel's God was the one true God.

In Joshua 2:9-11, Rahab confesses her faith:

"I know that the LORD has given you this land and that a great fear of you has fallen on us... We have heard how the LORD dried up the water of the Red Sea for you... for the LORD your God is God in heaven above and on the earth below."

This was not just an act of kindness. This was a declaration of faith.

She had not seen God's miracles firsthand. She had only heard about them.

But she believed.

And that faith saved her.

The Scarlet Cord – A Symbol of Redemption

Before the spies left, Rahab begged them to spare her life and the lives of her family when the Israelites conquered Jericho. The spies agreed and told her to tie a scarlet cord in her window as a sign.

That scarlet cord became a symbol of redemption—just like the blood of the Passover lamb had protected the Israelites in Egypt (Exodus 12:7), Rahab's home would be spared when destruction came to Jericho.

True to their word, when the walls of Jericho collapsed and the city was destroyed (Joshua 6), Rahab and her family were saved.

She went from being an outcast to being grafted into the people of God.

Rahab's Redemption – A Future She Never Imagined

Rahab could have lived out the rest of her days as an outsider—grateful to be spared but forever known as "that woman from Jericho."

But God had more for her.

She did not just join Israel; she became part of the lineage of Jesus Christ.

Matthew 1:5 tells us that Rahab married Salmon, a prince of Judah, and became the mother of Boaz—the great-grandfather of King David.

Think about that!

A woman who was once known as a prostitute became an ancestor of the Messiah.

This is the power of God's grace.

He does not just forgive—He redeems. He takes what the world sees as shameful and transforms it into something glorious.

The Power of Transformation Through Faith

Rahab's story reminds us that faith, not the past, defines our future.

The world would have seen Rahab as unworthy, sinful, and beyond hope. But God saw a woman of courage, a woman of faith, a woman willing to trust Him.

Throughout the Bible, we see other lives transformed by faith:

Moses was a murderer, but God made him a deliverer.

David was an adulterer, but God called him a man after His own heart.

Peter denied Jesus three times, but God made him the leader of the early church.

Paul persecuted Christians, but God turned him into one of the greatest apostles.

Rahab's name appears in Hebrews 11:31—the famous "Hall of Faith."

"By faith the prostitute Rahab, because she welcomed the spies, was not killed with those who were disobedient."

Her story teaches us that our past does not limit what God can do in our future.

Real-Life Examples – Stories of Redemption

Even today, God is still in the business of redeeming broken pasts.

There are countless testimonies of people who were once bound by sin, addiction, abuse, or failure but who encountered the grace of God and were transformed.

A former drug addict who is now a pastor, leading others to freedom in Christ.

A woman who was abandoned and broken but found healing in God's love and now helps others rebuild their lives.

A prisoner who committed terrible crimes but met Jesus in his cell and now ministers to others behind bars.

These stories remind us that God's grace is bigger than any mistake, any failure, and any past.

Your Story is Not Over

If you have ever felt like your past is too messy, too broken, or too far gone for God to use, let Rahab's story remind you:

God is not finished with you.

No matter where you've been, what you've done, or what others have said about you, God can write a new chapter in your life.
All He asks is for faith—the kind of faith that Rahab had.
Faith that believes in who He is.
Faith that trusts in His mercy.
Faith that says, "I may have a past, but God holds my future."

Reflection Questions

1. *Have you ever struggled to believe that God can use you despite your past mistakes?*
2. *What steps can you take to trust in God's ability to redeem and restore your life?*
3. *How does Rahab's faith challenge you to see beyond your circumstances?*
4. *Is there someone in your life who feels unworthy of God's love? How can you encourage them with Rahab's story?*
5. *What does the scarlet cord symbolize in your own journey of faith?*

Final Encouragement
Rahab's story is your story.
It is the story of grace, redemption, and the power of faith.
No matter where you have been, no matter what has happened in your past—God is not done with you.
All you have to do is trust Him.
And just like Rahab, you will see that a past full of brokenness cannot stop a future filled with God's purpose.

Miriam – The Dangers of Jealousy & the Role of a Worshiper

The story of Miriam is a powerful reminder that a person can be both anointed and flawed, a worshiper and yet vulnerable to jealousy, a leader yet still in need of humility.

Miriam's life is one of highs and lows, triumphs and failures, but through it all, we see the hand of God—teaching, correcting, and restoring. Her story holds deep lessons for every believer, especially those who serve in positions of leadership and influence.

It warns us of the dangers of pride and jealousy while showing us the true heart of a worshiper—one who exalts God above all, including personal ambition.

Miriam's Rise to Leadership

Miriam first appears in the book of Exodus, not as a great prophetess or leader, but as a young girl with great courage.

At a time when Pharaoh had issued a decree that all Hebrew baby boys should be drowned in the Nile, Miriam's mother, Jochebed, defied the order. She placed her infant son, Moses, in a basket and set him afloat on the river, entrusting him to God's care (Exodus 2:3).

It was Miriam who watched over her baby brother, waiting to see what would happen. When Pharaoh's daughter discovered the child, Miriam had the boldness to step forward and suggest that a Hebrew woman (her own mother) nurse him.

Even at a young age, Miriam demonstrated leadership, boldness, and a heart for God's people. She was not an ordinary girl—she was destined to be part of God's plan for Israel.

Fast forward many years, and Miriam had become a key figure in Israel. Alongside Moses and Aaron, she was a leader of the nation, guiding them out of Egypt toward the Promised Land.

In Exodus 15:20-21, after the miraculous parting of the Red Sea and Israel's deliverance from Egypt, Miriam leads the entire nation in worship.

"Then Miriam the prophetess, Aaron's sister, took a timbrel in her hand, and all the women followed her, with timbrels and dancing. Miriam sang to them: 'Sing to the LORD, for He is highly exalted. Both horse and driver He has hurled into the sea.'"

This was Miriam's highest moment—she was not just a worship leader; she was a prophetess, a voice of praise, a woman of great influence.

She had walked in faith and seen God's power firsthand.

But power can be dangerous when mixed with pride.

The Fall – When Jealousy Took Root

As time passed, Miriam's heart changed.

She had led worship, she had prophesied, she had been honored. But something happened in her heart—jealousy crept in.

In Numbers 12:1-2, we see a shocking turn in her story:

"Miriam and Aaron began to talk against Moses because of his Cushite wife, for he had married a Cushite. 'Has the LORD spoken only through Moses?' they asked. 'Hasn't He also spoken through us?' And the LORD heard this."

Miriam was no longer singing about God's greatness—now, she was complaining about Moses.

This was not just about his wife. At the root of it, Miriam was jealous. She had once been a key leader, but now, Moses was the one with greater authority. God spoke to Moses face to face (Numbers 12:6-8), while she and Aaron received revelation differently.

Instead of rejoicing in God's calling on her brother's life, she resented it.

Instead of honoring the role God had given her, she wanted more.

She forgot something important: Leadership is not about position—it's about submission.

God's Response – A Hard Lesson in Humility

Miriam's jealousy did not go unnoticed. The Lord heard her complaints—and He was not pleased.

In Numbers 12:4-10, God summoned Miriam, Aaron, and Moses to the Tent of Meeting.

There, He made it clear:

"When there is a prophet among you, I, the LORD, reveal Myself to them in visions… But this is not true of My servant Moses; with him, I speak face to face." (Numbers 12:6-8)

Then, God's judgment fell upon Miriam.

When the presence of the Lord lifted, Miriam was covered in leprosy. Her skin turned white, a physical representation of the spiritual sickness that had taken root in her heart.

Aaron immediately repented, recognizing their sin, and pleaded with Moses to intercede for Miriam.

And here's the beauty of Moses' heart—he prayed for her.

Even though Miriam had opposed him, Moses did not rejoice in her downfall. Instead, he cried out to God:

"Please, God, heal her!" (Numbers 12:13)

God, in His mercy, healed her—but she was required to stay outside the camp for seven days as a consequence of her actions.

The Importance of Humility in Leadership

Miriam's story teaches us that pride and jealousy can destroy even the most anointed people.

She had been a leader, a worshiper, a prophetess—but the moment she let jealousy take root, it nearly destroyed her.

Pride is dangerous because it blinds us to our own faults.

Jealousy is destructive because it makes us resent the blessings of others instead of celebrating them.

Leadership isn't about competing—it's about serving.

Jesus, the greatest leader of all, said:

"Whoever wants to become great among you must be your servant." (Matthew 20:26)

True worship is not just about singing songs—it's about having a heart that is humble before God.

Real-Life Example – Handling Success Without Pride

Even today, we see many leaders struggle with success.

A pastor starts his ministry in humility, but as his influence grows, pride begins to creep in.

A worship leader begins by pointing people to Jesus, but over time, it becomes about their talent and recognition.

A business leader who once relied on God now thinks they are self-made.

Success can be a test as much as failure.

The question is: Will we remain humble?

Miriam's story warns us: No one is immune to pride.

Even those closest to God must guard their hearts.

Final Lessons from Miriam's Life

A true worshiper exalts God, not themselves.

Jealousy is dangerous—it can rob us of our calling.

Leadership is not about position; it's about humility.

Even when we fall, God is merciful—but sin has consequences.
Success is not about how high you go, but how low you are willing to bow before God.

Reflection Questions

1. *Have you ever struggled with jealousy or comparison? How can you surrender that to God?*
2. *What steps can you take to ensure that success doesn't lead to pride in your life?*
3. *Do you celebrate the gifts and callings of others, or do you feel resentment when others are promoted?*
4. *How does Miriam's story challenge you in your walk with God?*
5. *What does it truly mean to be a worshiper beyond just singing?*

Final Encouragement:
Miriam's story is both a warning and an encouragement.
It reminds us that God can use us greatly, but we must always guard our hearts against pride and jealousy.
No matter how high we rise, our role is always to worship God, not ourselves.
Will you remain a humble worshiper?

Section 2:
The Fulfillment of Womanhood (New Testament Women)

Mary (Mother of Jesus) – The Ultimate Surrender

The story of Mary, the mother of Jesus, is one of the greatest testimonies of faith, trust, and surrender in the entire Bible.

Mary was a young girl—likely in her early teens—when she was visited by the angel Gabriel with a message that would change her life forever. She had her own dreams, her own plans for the future. Yet, in a moment, everything shifted. She had a choice: hold on to her plans or surrender completely to God's purpose.

Her response?

"I am the Lord's servant… May your word to me be fulfilled." (Luke 1:38)

With those words of surrender, she stepped into the most significant calling in human history—to carry and give birth to the Son of God.

But surrender is never easy. It often requires us to let go of certainty, to walk paths we never expected, and to trust even when we don't understand.

Mary's life is a powerful reminder that true faith is not just believing in God, but yielding to Him completely—even when it doesn't make sense.

A Divine Interruption – The Call to Surrender

Mary was just an ordinary girl. She was betrothed to Joseph, preparing for marriage, anticipating a simple and honorable life as a wife in a small town.

Then, suddenly, an angel appeared.

"Greetings, you who are highly favored! The Lord is with you." (Luke 1:28)

The words startled her. Who was she that an angel would call her *"highly favored"?*

The message Gabriel delivered was unimaginable: *"You will conceive and give birth to a son, and you are to call him Jesus. He will be great and will be called the Son of the Most High."* (Luke 1:31-32)

Mary was confused. How could this be?

"How will this be," Mary asked, "since I am a virgin?" (Luke 1:34)

It wasn't doubt. It was genuine wonder—a girl trying to make sense of something impossible.

Gabriel assured her:

"The Holy Spirit will come upon you, and the power of the Most High will overshadow you. So the holy one to be born will be called the Son of God." (Luke 1:35)

And then, the angel added something even more remarkable—news that should have been impossible:

"Even Elizabeth, your relative, is going to have a child in her old age, and she who was said to be unable to conceive is in her sixth month. For no word from God will ever fail." (Luke 1:36-37)

It was a reminder that God specializes in the impossible.

Mary had a choice.

She could resist. She could argue. She could hesitate, worrying about what Joseph would say, what her parents would think, what the people in her village would do.

Instead, she simply said:

"I am the Lord's servant… May your word to me be fulfilled." (Luke 1:38)

Complete surrender. No conditions. No hesitation. Just faith.

Trusting God's Plan When It Doesn't Make Sense

Mary's surrender wasn't without cost.

She was not yet married—yet now she would be pregnant. In her culture, this could mean public shame, rejection, and even death by stoning.

Joseph, her fiancé, would naturally assume she had been unfaithful. Would he leave her? Would she be disgraced?

Yet Mary trusted God.

When Joseph discovered Mary was pregnant, he did consider leaving her (Matthew 1:19). Yet, because he was a righteous man, he planned to do so quietly to avoid exposing her to shame.

But then, God intervened.

An angel appeared to Joseph in a dream, revealing the truth:

"Do not be afraid to take Mary home as your wife, because what is conceived in her is from the Holy Spirit." (Matthew 1:20)

Joseph obeyed, and Mary's surrender was met with God's provision.

But this was only the beginning.

Even after Jesus was born, Mary's life was filled with uncertainties:

- ✓ Fleeing to Egypt to escape King Herod's massacre (Matthew 2:13-15).
- ✓ Raising the Son of God, knowing one day He would leave her.
- ✓ Watching her son die on a cross—the most painful experience any mother could endure.

She didn't always understand. At times, she pondered things in her heart (Luke 2:19, 51), trying to grasp the weight of her calling.

Yet, she never took back her "yes."

Even at the cross, when it seemed like all hope was lost, Mary stood there, steadfast in her surrender.

And three days later, her faith was rewarded. Her Son rose from the grave, proving that God's plans are always greater than we can imagine.

Surrendering Our Own Plans for God's Purpose

Mary's story is not just a historical account—it is an invitation.

Every believer is called to a moment of surrender, where God interrupts our plans and asks us to trust Him.

For some, it's leaving behind a career to follow God's call.

For others, it's stepping out in faith even when the road ahead is uncertain.

Even today, we see countless women who, like Mary, surrender their plans to God's purpose.

- ✓ A woman who dreams of a successful career but chooses to be a missionary.
- ✓ A mother who raises God-fearing children instead of pursuing worldly success.
- ✓ A young woman who says "yes" to purity, even when the world pressures her otherwise.
- ✓ A wife who prays faithfully for her husband's salvation instead of walking away.

Surrender is not always easy.

But Mary's life proves that it is always worth it.

Final Lessons from Mary's Life

God's calling is often unexpected. He chooses ordinary people for extraordinary purposes.

Surrender requires trust. Mary didn't know all the answers, but she trusted the One who did.

Faithfulness in surrender leads to blessings. God provided for Mary at every step.

Even in pain, God's purpose prevails. Mary endured suffering, but she also witnessed resurrection.

No surrender to God is ever wasted. What seemed like a loss—giving up her plans—was actually the greatest honor.

Reflection Questions

1. *Are there areas in your life where you struggle to surrender to God's plan? What holds you back?*
2. *How can Mary's story encourage you to trust God, even when things don't make sense?*
3. *Have you ever had a moment where God asked you to give up your plans for something greater? What was your response?*
4. *What is one step of surrender you can take today in your faith journey?*
5. *In what ways can you, like Mary, say "Yes" to God in your daily life?*

Final Encouragement

Mary's surrender changed history.
And your surrender—no matter how small or unseen—can change lives too.
When you say "yes" to God, you are stepping into something far greater than you can imagine.
Will you trust Him? Will you surrender?
Because when you do, you will see the impossible become possible.

Elizabeth – Faithfulness in the Waiting

Waiting is one of the hardest things we ever have to do. In a world that values speed, instant results, and quick fixes, waiting feels like wasted time. Yet, in God's kingdom, waiting is not passive—it is an active posture of faith, trust, and preparation.

The story of Elizabeth, the mother of John the Baptist, is a beautiful example of faithfulness in the waiting. She and her husband, Zechariah, had prayed for years for a child, yet the years passed, and nothing happened.

By the time we meet them in Luke's Gospel, Elizabeth is old, her hair likely streaked with silver, her body past the natural age of childbearing. To the world, hope was gone.

And yet, in the waiting, God was working.

Because when the answer finally came, it was not just a child—it was a prophet, a forerunner to the Messiah, the one who would prepare the way for the Lord.

Elizabeth's story teaches us that delays are not denials, that waiting is not punishment, and that God's timing is always perfect.

A Life of Longing – Trusting God's Promise Despite Delays

Elizabeth was a righteous woman—faithful to God, committed to His commandments. She and Zechariah were descendants of Aaron, coming from a priestly line, and their lives were marked by devotion to the Lord (Luke 1:5-6).

Yet, despite their righteousness, they had no child.

In Jewish culture, barrenness was deeply painful—not just emotionally but socially. A woman without children was often viewed as cursed or forgotten by God. Neighbors would whisper, extended family would talk, and even well-meaning friends might offer empty words of comfort.

Perhaps Elizabeth had once clung to hope—counting the days, watching for signs of pregnancy, praying through tears. But with every passing year, the dream faded.

And yet, Elizabeth never turned bitter.

She remained faithful—serving, trusting, worshiping, even when the heavens seemed silent.

Then, everything changed.

One day, while Zechariah was serving in the temple, an angel appeared.

"Do not be afraid, Zechariah; your prayer has been heard. Your wife Elizabeth will bear you a son, and you are to call him John." (Luke 1:13)

The words were unbelievable—so much so that Zechariah himself doubted.

"How can I be sure of this? I am an old man, and my wife is well along in years." (Luke 1:18)

Because of his doubt, Zechariah was struck mute until the child was born.

But Elizabeth?

Her response was different.

When she became pregnant, her first words were not of doubt, but of gratitude.

"The Lord has done this for me… In these days he has shown his favor and taken away my disgrace among the people." (Luke 1:25)

She recognized that the waiting had a purpose.

She saw the faithfulness of God.

And she understood that even when it seemed like God was delaying, He had never forgotten her.

The Blessing of Waiting on God's Timing

Elizabeth's story reminds us that waiting is not wasted time.

If John had been born years earlier, he would not have been the prophet that prepared the way for Jesus. His birth had to align with God's plan—just before the Messiah entered the world.

God was not just preparing Elizabeth and Zechariah. He was preparing history itself.

How often do we think that God's delays are rejections?

We pray for healing, for breakthrough, for open doors—and when nothing happens, we assume God has forgotten.

But Elizabeth's life teaches us that when the time is right, the answer will come.

And when it does, it will be far greater than we ever imagined.

Consider Abraham and Sarah.

They, too, waited for a child—decades of longing, of hoping, of questioning.

Sarah, like Elizabeth, was barren. But when the angel of the Lord visited Abraham, He gave a promise:

"I will surely return to you about this time next year, and Sarah your wife will have a son." (Genesis 18:10)

Sarah laughed—not out of joy, but out of disbelief.

"After I am worn out and my lord is old, will I now have this pleasure?" (Genesis 18:12)

But God's response was clear:

"Is anything too hard for the Lord?" (Genesis 18:14)

Just as Sarah conceived Isaac in her old age, Elizabeth conceived John—both reminders that God's promises do not expire.

If He has spoken it, it will come to pass.

Real-Life Example: Women Experiencing Delayed Answers to Prayer

Even today, so many women walk in Elizabeth's footsteps.

A woman praying for a child, year after year, yet still waiting.

A mother praying for her prodigal son to return to the faith, yet still watching from a distance.

A single woman praying for a godly husband, yet still waiting for God's best.

A wife praying for her husband's heart to soften toward the Lord, yet still seeing no change.

The waiting is painful.

The silence is heavy.

And yet, God is faithful.

I know a woman who waited over a decade to have a child. She prayed, cried, and wrestled with God. There were moments she wanted to give up. But at just the right time, God opened her womb—and she became a mother to a beautiful baby girl.

And the best part?

Because of the years she spent waiting, her faith had grown so deep that she now ministers to other women facing the same struggles.

Her waiting wasn't wasted.

Neither was Elizabeth's.

Neither is yours.

Final Encouragement

Elizabeth's story is a reminder that God never forgets His promises.

You may be in a season of waiting—for a breakthrough, a relationship, a miracle.
You may feel like time has run out.
But let this truth sink deep into your heart:
God is never late. He is always on time.
And when the answer comes, it will be worth every second of the wait.

Reflection Questions

1. *Have you ever felt like God was delaying something in your life? How did you respond?*
2. *What lessons from Elizabeth's story encourage you to trust God in your waiting?*
3. *In what ways can you remain faithful while you wait for God's promises to unfold?*
4. *How can you encourage someone else who is struggling in a season of waiting?*
5. *What is one promise from God's Word that you can hold onto today as you wait?*

Final Thought

Waiting is not easy. But God sees you, hears you, and remembers you.
Keep trusting. Keep believing.
Because when the answer finally comes, it will be greater than you ever imagined.

Mary Magdalene – Devotion That Transforms

Some encounters change a person forever.

For Mary Magdalene, meeting Jesus was not just a turning point—it was a resurrection of her very soul.

She is one of the most misunderstood figures in the Bible. For centuries, people have wrongly assumed she was a prostitute, though Scripture never states that. What we do know is this: she was a woman who had been completely bound by darkness, and Jesus set her free.

Mary Magdalene's story is one of radical transformation, relentless devotion, and a love that refused to let go. She went from a life of torment to becoming the first witness of the greatest event in history—the Resurrection of Jesus Christ.

A Life Bound by Darkness

When Mary Magdalene first appears in the Gospels, her life is in utter chaos.

Luke 8:2 tells us that she had been possessed by seven demons—a description that speaks to deep spiritual torment.

Imagine her condition:

- ✓ Tormented, day and night.
- ✓ Rejected by society, feared by her own people.
- ✓ Trapped in a prison she could not escape.

We don't know what these demons caused her to do—whether they filled her mind with terror, drove her to self-harm, or made her an outcast. But we know this: she was utterly helpless.

Until Jesus.

He spoke a word, and the torment stopped.

He extended His hand, and the chains fell off.
He looked into her eyes, and for the first time in years, she saw hope.
The same Jesus who calmed the raging sea had now calmed the raging storm within her soul.
And from that moment, she never left Him.

A Devotion That Knew No Limits

Mary Magdalene was not just a follower of Jesus—she was one of His most devoted disciples.
While others came and went, she stayed.
Luke 8:3 tells us that she, along with other women, helped financially support Jesus' ministry. She wasn't just following Jesus for what He could do for her—she gave her life to serve Him.
This is what true transformation looks like.

- ✓ When you have been set free, you don't want to go back.
- ✓ When you have been rescued, you want to tell the world.
- ✓ When you have encountered true love, you never want to leave.

Her devotion was so deep that even in Jesus' darkest hour, she remained.
While His disciples fled in fear, Mary Magdalene was there.
She stood at the foot of the cross, watching as her Savior bled and died (John 19:25).
When Joseph of Arimathea buried Him, she followed to see where His body was laid (Matthew 27:61).
And on the morning of the third day, while it was still dark, she ran to His tomb—not because she expected a resurrection, but because she just wanted to be near Him, even in death (John 20:1).
That's devotion.
That's love.

And because of that love, she received the greatest honor in human history.

The First Witness of the Resurrection

In John 20, we find one of the most emotional moments in all of Scripture.

Mary comes to the tomb and finds it empty. Jesus is gone.

Heartbroken, she assumes someone has stolen His body.

She stays outside, weeping.

Suddenly, she sees someone standing near her, but she doesn't recognize Him.

"Woman, why are you crying? Who is it you are looking for?" (John 20:15)

She thinks He is the gardener.

"Sir, if you have carried Him away, tell me where you have put Him, and I will get Him."

Then, Jesus speaks one word.

"Mary."

And in that instant, she knows.

She turns to Him and cries out, "Rabboni!" (which means "Teacher").

He is alive.

Jesus did not reveal Himself first to Peter. Not to John. Not even to His own mother.

He chose Mary Magdalene—a once-broken woman who had been restored by His love.

Why?

Because Jesus honors devotion.

He reveals Himself to those who are hungry, desperate, and faithful.

And through this moment, Mary became the first evangelist in history—carrying the message of the Resurrection to the disciples.

"I have seen the Lord!" (John 20:18)

She who was once bound by darkness now became a bearer of the greatest light.

True Freedom Comes Through Jesus

Mary Magdalene's story is a testimony that no one is too broken for Jesus to restore.

The enemy may have had a stronghold in her life, but Jesus had the final say.

This pattern of redemption is seen all throughout Scripture.

- ✓ The Israelites in Egypt – For 400 years, they were slaves in bondage. Yet, when the time came, God sent Moses to lead them into freedom (Exodus 3:7-8).
- ✓ Hannah, the barren woman – She wept in the temple, crying out for a child. In her brokenness, she made a vow to God, and in time, she gave birth to Samuel, one of Israel's greatest prophets (1 Samuel 1:10-20).
- ✓ The woman with the issue of blood – She suffered for twelve years, spending everything she had on doctors. But one touch of Jesus' garment, and her suffering ended instantly (Mark 5:25-34).

In every case, Jesus is the one who brings true freedom.

And He is still doing it today.

Real-Life Example: Women Restored from Brokenness

I once met a woman who had been in abusive relationships for years. She believed she was worthless, trapped in a cycle of pain.

One night, she cried out to Jesus in desperation.

Something changed.

A peace she had never known filled her heart.

Over time, she walked away from those toxic situations. She found healing, restoration, and purpose.

Today, she helps other women break free from abuse and discover their identity in Christ.

Her life is a testimony of what Mary Magdalene experienced:

Bondage does not have the final word.

Jesus does.

Final Encouragement

Mary Magdalene's life is proof that Jesus doesn't just save us—He transforms us.

If you feel broken, lost, or unworthy, take heart.

The same Jesus who called Mary by name calls you too.

And when you surrender to Him, your story will never be the same.

Reflection Questions

1. *What areas of your life still feel bound, and how can you bring them to Jesus for healing?*
2. *How does Mary Magdalene's devotion challenge you in your own faith?*
3. *Have you ever felt unworthy of God's love? How does her story encourage you?*
4. *In what ways has Jesus transformed your life, and how can you share that testimony with others?*
5. *What does it mean for you to be a witness of the Resurrection in your daily life?*

Final Thought

Jesus didn't just set Mary free—He gave her a new purpose. And He is ready to do the same for you.

Will you answer His call?

The Woman with the Issue of Blood – Faith That Pushes Through

Some moments define a life.
For twelve long years, she had been suffering—physically, emotionally, socially, and spiritually.
She was a woman living in the shadows, carrying an affliction that made her an outcast. Every doctor had failed her, every treatment had drained her resources, and every passing year had whispered a cruel message: "There is no hope for you."
But then, she heard about Jesus.
Something stirred in her heart.
Hope—faint but determined—began to rise.
And that day, as Jesus passed through her town, she did something extraordinary.
She pushed through.
She defied the voices that told her she was unworthy.
She ignored the shame that tried to silence her.
She pressed forward in faith—and in doing so, she found her healing.
Her story is a powerful testament to what happens when faith refuses to give up.

A Life of Desperation

Mark 5:25-26 paints a tragic picture:
"And a woman was there who had been subject to bleeding for twelve years. She had suffered a great deal under the care of many doctors and had spent all she had, yet instead of getting better she grew worse."
This woman's condition was more than just a medical issue—it was a life sentence of isolation.

In Jewish law, any woman who had continuous bleeding was considered unclean (Leviticus 15:25-27). This meant:

- ✓ She couldn't enter the temple to worship.
- ✓ She couldn't be touched by anyone—including her own family.
- ✓ She was socially and religiously outcast, living in shame.

Twelve years.
Can you imagine?
Twelve years of rejection.
Twelve years of people avoiding her, whispering about her.
Twelve years of praying for a miracle that never seemed to come.
Many would have given up.
Many would have accepted their fate.
But this woman still had faith—a faith that was bruised, battered, but still alive.
And when she heard that Jesus was near, something inside her refused to stay silent.
"If I just touch His clothes, I will be healed." (Mark 5:28)
That was all she needed.
Not His full attention.
Not a long conversation.
Not even an invitation.
Just one touch.

Faith That Pushes Through

The streets were packed. A crowd surrounded Jesus, pressing against Him on every side.
It would have been easy to turn back.
To say, "It's too crowded."
To think, "What if someone recognizes me and shames me?"

To fear, "What if this doesn't work?"
But desperate faith does not stop at obstacles.
She pushed through the crowd—weak, frail, but determined.
She stretched out her hand—unnoticed, unseen, but full of expectation.
And in an instant, her world changed.
"Immediately her bleeding stopped, and she felt in her body that she was freed from her suffering." (Mark 5:29)
After twelve years of agony, the pain vanished in a moment.
Jesus didn't even touch her.
It was her faith that reached out and took hold of His power.
And then—something incredible happened.
Jesus Turns and Sees Her
Jesus, surrounded by a crushing crowd, stopped.
He turned around and asked:
"Who touched me?" (Mark 5:30)
The disciples were confused. Everyone was touching Him.
But only one person had touched Him in faith.
She could have slipped away quietly—healed, whole, and unnoticed.
But Jesus didn't let that happen.
He wanted her to step forward.
Not to shame her, but to honor her.
Trembling, she fell at His feet and told Him the whole truth.
And instead of rebuking her, Jesus affirmed her faith:
"Daughter, your faith has healed you. Go in peace and be freed from your suffering." (Mark 5:34)
This was the only time in Scripture that Jesus called someone "Daughter."

It was personal.
It was intimate.
It was as if He was saying, "You are not an outcast anymore. You are My beloved child."

The Power of Persistent Faith

This woman's faith teaches us a vital truth:
Faith that pushes through the obstacles is the faith that receives the miracle.
Her healing wasn't just about physical restoration—it was about spiritual restoration.
She wasn't just healed—she was seen, loved, and accepted by Jesus.
The Bible is filled with stories of people who refused to give up:

- ✓ Hannah – She prayed year after year for a child, despite ridicule and barrenness, until God gave her Samuel (1 Samuel 1:10-20).
- ✓ Jacob – He wrestled with God all night and refused to let go until he received a blessing (Genesis 32:24-28).
- ✓ Blind Bartimaeus – He cried out for Jesus, even when people told him to be quiet. He refused to stop until Jesus healed him (Mark 10:46-52).

In each case, faith pushed through.
And in each case, God answered.

Real-Life Example: Women Overcoming Chronic Struggles

I once knew a woman who battled a severe illness for years.
Doctors gave her medication, but nothing seemed to work.
She felt forgotten, even by God.
But she kept praying.
She kept believing.

One day, she attended a service where people were being prayed for.
She felt something urging her to step forward.
In faith, she pushed through her fear, walked to the front, and asked for prayer.
And in that moment, she felt a warmth flood her body.
The illness that had plagued her for years? Gone.
She was healed.
Just like the woman in Mark 5, her faith had pushed through—and received a miracle.

Final Encouragement

What are you struggling with today?
Is it a chronic illness? A painful past? A prayer that seems unanswered?
Don't give up.
Push through the crowd.
Push past the doubt.
Because when you stretch out your hand in faith, Jesus is there.
And just like He did for that woman, He will stop, turn, and call you "Daughter."

Reflection Questions

1. *What are the obstacles in your life that are keeping you from fully reaching out to Jesus?*
2. *Have you ever felt like giving up on a prayer? How does this story encourage you to keep believing?*
3. *What does it mean to have faith that pushes through in your daily struggles?*
4. *In what ways have you experienced Jesus seeing and acknowledging you in your brokenness?*

5. *How can you encourage others who are waiting on their breakthrough?*

Final Thought

The woman with the issue of blood was not just healed—she was restored.
And the same Jesus who saw her sees you today.
Will you push through and reach for Him?

The Samaritan Woman – Evangelism Through Personal Testimony

Some encounters change everything.
She wasn't looking for salvation that day. She wasn't searching for healing or trying to find the Messiah.
She was simply going to get water.
It was an ordinary day at an ordinary well.
And yet, by the time she left, her entire life had changed.
The Samaritan woman is one of the most powerful examples in Scripture of how an encounter with Jesus restores identity and purpose—and how a transformed life becomes the greatest testimony.
She came to the well as an outcast.
She left as a revivalist.

The Woman at the Well – A Life of Rejection

It was noon, the hottest part of the day, when the Samaritan woman made her way to Jacob's well.
Most women came to draw water in the early morning or late evening, when it was cooler.
But she came alone.
This small detail speaks volumes.
She wasn't welcome among the other women.
She wasn't part of their conversations, their laughter, or their shared burdens.
She carried a different burden—one of shame, of whispered rumors, of glances filled with judgment.
Her past was an open scandal in her small town.
She had been married five times, and the man she was currently with wasn't even her husband (John 4:18).
For most people, her story would have ended there.
Just another woman with a broken past.

Just another person stuck in the cycle of mistakes and regrets.

But that day, at the well, Jesus was waiting for her.

And He never lets a broken story go to waste.

An Unlikely Conversation

"Will you give me a drink?" (John 4:7)

Jesus could have performed a miracle on the spot. He could have commanded water to rise from the well or preached a sermon.

Instead, He asked for a drink.

In doing so, He broke two major barriers:

- ✓ A Jew speaking to a Samaritan.
  Jews and Samaritans hated each other. Their divisions ran deep, rooted in history, politics, and religion. No Jewish man would have voluntarily spoken to a Samaritan woman.
- ✓ A rabbi speaking to a woman with a tainted past.
  Jewish teachers did not speak to women in public, let alone one with a reputation. She was the kind of person religious leaders avoided.

And yet, Jesus pursued a conversation with her.

Why?

Because He wasn't there for water.

He was there for her.

He saw beyond her outward failures and into her inner thirst.

She came to the well for water.

But He came to the well to give her something far greater.

The Living Water – Identity Restored

The woman was intrigued but skeptical.

"Sir, you have nothing to draw with, and the well is deep. Where can you get this living water?" (John 4:11)

She didn't understand at first.

She was thinking about physical water, but Jesus was talking about something eternal.

"Everyone who drinks this water will be thirsty again, but whoever drinks the water I give them will never thirst. Indeed, the water I give them will become in them a spring of water welling up to eternal life." (John 4:13-14)

Jesus wasn't just offering forgiveness—He was offering a new identity.

She wasn't too broken.

She wasn't too sinful.

She wasn't too far gone.

She had been searching for satisfaction in relationships, in acceptance, in human love.

But only Jesus could quench the thirst of her soul.

A Divine Revelation

Then, Jesus did something extraordinary.

He revealed who He truly was.

"I know that Messiah is coming," she said. "When he comes, he will explain everything to us." (John 4:25)

Then Jesus declared:

"I, the one speaking to you—I am He." (John 4:26)

This was the first recorded instance in Scripture where Jesus openly declared His identity as the Messiah.

And He chose a Samaritan woman with a sinful past as the first to hear it.

From Outcast to Revivalist

The moment the woman understood who Jesus was, she left her water jar and ran into town.

She didn't walk.

She didn't hesitate.
She ran.
And what was her message?
"Come, see a man who told me everything I ever did. Could this be the Messiah?" (John 4:29)
The very things that had once shamed her—her past, her mistakes, her brokenness—became her testimony.
She wasn't a theologian.
She wasn't a preacher.
She wasn't even fully healed from her past.
But she had met Jesus, and that was enough.
And because of her, an entire town came to Christ.
"Many of the Samaritans from that town believed in Him because of the woman's testimony." (John 4:39)
She came to the well as an outcast—and left as a revivalist.

God's Pattern – Using the Unlikely

This is the pattern of God's grace.
He takes the unqualified, the broken, the outcast—and makes them His messengers.
We see this throughout Scripture:

- ✓ Moses was a fugitive and a stutterer, yet God called him to lead Israel (Exodus 3:11-12).
- ✓ Rahab was a prostitute, yet she became part of Jesus' genealogy (Matthew 1:5).
- ✓ David was an adulterer, yet God called him a man after His own heart (Acts 13:22).
- ✓ Paul was a murderer of Christians, yet he became one of the greatest apostles (1 Timothy 1:15-16).

The Samaritan woman's story reminds us of this truth:
Your past does not disqualify you from God's purpose.

In fact, it may be the very thing He uses to bring others to Him.

Real-Life Example: Women Leading in Ministry Despite Pasts

I once met a woman who had spent years caught in addiction.

She had made mistakes.

She had hurt people.

She believed she would never be worthy of ministry.

But then, she had an encounter with Jesus.

He didn't just forgive her—He restored her.

Today, she leads a women's ministry, helping others find healing from the very struggles she once faced.

Her past didn't disqualify her.

It prepared her.

And just like the Samaritan woman, her testimony has led many to Jesus.

Final Encouragement

No matter what your past looks like, Jesus is not done with you.

Your story is not over.

And your testimony may be the very thing that brings someone else to Christ.

Will you let Him use you?

Reflection Questions

1. *Have you ever felt like your past disqualifies you from God's purpose? How does this story change that perspective?*
2. *What "water jars" in your life—old patterns, burdens, or shame—do you need to leave behind?*
3. *How has Jesus transformed your life in a way that could be a testimony to others?*

4. *Who in your life needs to hear about what Jesus has done for you?*

Your testimony is powerful.
Let Jesus use it to change lives—just like He did with the Samaritan woman.

The Persistent Widow – The Power of Unyielding Prayer

Some prayers are answered in an instant—like a flash of lightning illuminating the night.

Others take time, testing our faith, stretching our endurance, and refining our hearts in the waiting.

Jesus knew that persistence in prayer is one of the greatest demonstrations of faith. That's why He told the parable of the persistent widow—a woman who refused to take no for an answer.

She was relentless.

She was unwavering.

She was determined.

And in the end, her persistence moved the heart of an unjust judge.

If a corrupt man could be persuaded by perseverance, how much more will our righteous and loving God respond to those who seek Him without ceasing?

This is the power of unyielding prayer.

A Widow Who Refused to Give Up

The parable in Luke 18:1-8 is short, but its message is profound.

Jesus begins by telling His disciples why He is sharing this story:

"Then Jesus told His disciples a parable to show them that they should always pray and not give up." (Luke 18:1)

Right from the start, we see the heart of God—He wants us to keep praying, keep believing, and never quit.

The story unfolds with a widow who kept coming to a judge, pleading:

"Grant me justice against my adversary!" (Luke 18:3)
We don't know the details of her case.
We don't know what injustice she suffered.
But what we do know is this:
She was alone in a world that favored the powerful.
Widows in biblical times had little to no rights. Without a husband, father, or son to speak on her behalf, she had no social standing.
Yet she did not let that stop her.
She knocked.
She pleaded.
She came back again and again.
The judge, on the other hand, was the worst kind of authority figure.
"He neither feared God nor cared what people thought." (Luke 18:2)
He was corrupt, indifferent, and uninterested in justice.
For a long time, he refused to help her.
But eventually, her persistence wore him down.
"Even though I don't fear God or care what people think, yet because this widow keeps bothering me, I will see that she gets justice, so that she won't eventually come and attack me!" (Luke 18:4-5)
The unjust judge only acted out of selfishness—he wanted her to stop bothering him.
But Jesus wasn't comparing God to this judge; He was making a contrast.
If a man so wicked could be moved by persistence, how much more will our loving Father respond to His children when they cry out to Him day and night?
Jesus ends the parable with a promise and a challenge:
"And will not God bring about justice for His chosen ones, who cry out to Him day and night? Will He

keep putting them off? I tell you, He will see that they get justice, and quickly." (Luke 18:7-8)
God is not like the unjust judge—He is faithful, good, and full of mercy.
And yet, Jesus leaves us with a powerful question:
"However, when the Son of Man comes, will He find faith on the earth?" (Luke 18:8)
Will He find a generation that still believes in the power of prayer?
Will He find people who refuse to give up?
Persistence in Spiritual Battles
The Bible is filled with stories of those who had to fight in prayer before they saw victory.
One of the greatest examples is Daniel.
In Daniel 10, we read that he prayed and fasted for 21 days before an angel appeared to him with an answer.
The angel said something remarkable:
"Since the first day that you set your mind to gain understanding and to humble yourself before your God, your words were heard, and I have come in response to them." (Daniel 10:12)
Daniel's prayer was answered the moment he began praying—but there was a spiritual battle delaying the response.
"But the prince of the Persian kingdom resisted me twenty-one days." (Daniel 10:13)
Daniel did not stop praying, even though he saw no immediate results.
His persistence broke through the resistance in the spiritual realm.
What if he had given up on day 20?
What if his breakthrough was one more prayer away?
Many times, we quit too soon.

We assume silence means God is not listening, when in reality, He is working behind the scenes in ways we cannot see.

Real-Life Example: Women Interceding for Family, Community, and Nations

I once knew a mother who prayed for her son for 20 years.

He was addicted, rebellious, and lost.

Many people told her to give up, to stop hoping.

But she refused.

She prayed every morning.

She prayed every night.

She wept before God, believing for a miracle.

And then—after two decades of prayer—her son walked into a church, surrendered his life to Jesus, and was radically transformed.

That same son became a pastor.

She never stopped praying—and because of her persistence, an entire family was changed.

This is the power of unyielding prayer.

It can change hearts.

It can break addictions.

It can bring revival to entire nations.

Hannah: A Woman Who Refused to Be Silent

Hannah in the Old Testament is another powerful example of a woman who prayed persistently.

She was barren, mocked, and brokenhearted.

Yet, year after year, she went to the temple, pouring out her soul before the Lord (1 Samuel 1:10-11).

She was so desperate in prayer that Eli the priest thought she was drunk!

But God heard her cry—and she gave birth to Samuel, one of the greatest prophets in Israel's history.

Her persistence changed the course of an entire nation.

Final Encouragement

The enemy's greatest strategy is to make you give up too soon.
To whisper:
"Nothing is happening."
"God isn't listening."
"You've prayed enough."
But the truth is—every prayer you pray matters.
Even when you don't see it.
Even when you don't feel it.
Even when everything around you says, "Give up."
God is faithful.
And He is looking for people who will keep praying until the breakthrough comes.
Will you be one of them?

Reflection Questions

1. *Have you ever stopped praying for something because you felt like God wasn't answering? What does this story teach you about persistence?*
2. *What is one situation in your life that requires unwavering prayer right now?*
3. *Daniel's breakthrough was delayed due to spiritual warfare. Could there be unseen battles affecting your answered prayers? How does that change your perspective?*
4. *Who in your life needs you to intercede for them?*

Never stop praying.

Your breakthrough may be closer than you think.

Phoebe – Serving with Excellence in the Church

There are names in the Bible that are often overlooked, hidden like gems waiting to be discovered. Phoebe is one of those names. Though only briefly mentioned in Paul's letter to the Romans, her impact and legacy are undeniable.

She was not a preacher. She was not an apostle. But she was a servant, a leader, a deacon, and a woman of excellence—one whom Paul personally entrusted with carrying and delivering his most theologically rich letter, the Epistle to the Romans.

Her life was a testimony to what it means to serve God with distinction, faithfulness, and honor. And today, her story still speaks—calling us to embrace the heart of servanthood with excellence.

Phoebe: A Woman Highly Esteemed

Paul's words in Romans 16:1-2 introduce us to Phoebe:

"I commend to you our sister Phoebe, a deacon of the church in Cenchreae. I ask you to receive her in the Lord in a way worthy of His people and to give her any help she may need from you, for she has been the benefactor of many people, including me."

In these few sentences, we learn three powerful things about Phoebe:

- ✓ She was a deacon in the church at Cenchreae.
- ✓ Paul personally commended her and asked the church in Rome to support her.
- ✓ She was a benefactor, meaning she used her resources to support the ministry.

Each of these points tells us who she was, what she did, and why she mattered in the early church.

A Deacon with a Purpose

The word *deacon* comes from the Greek *diakonos*, which means servant or minister. Deacons were chosen for their character, faithfulness, and dedication to helping the church function smoothly.

Phoebe was not merely a helper; she was entrusted with responsibility.

She was likely involved in:

- ✓ Organizing and assisting in the needs of the congregation
- ✓ Supporting traveling missionaries and apostles like Paul
- ✓ Serving in administrative and financial roles to help sustain the church

Her service was not secondary—it was essential.

Paul saw her as worthy of honor and publicly acknowledged her leadership, showing us that women played significant roles in the early church.

The Importance of Supporting Ministry and Leadership

Phoebe's example teaches us something powerful:

Ministry is not just about preaching—it is about serving.

Many people admire the apostles and evangelists, but behind every great movement of God are people like Phoebe—faithful servants who support, organize, and sustain the work of the Kingdom.

Jesus Himself said:

"Whoever wants to become great among you must be your servant." (Matthew 20:26)

True greatness is not about position—it is about servanthood.

This is why Paul urged the Roman church to receive Phoebe "in a way worthy of His people."
She was not just another believer—she was a leader, a supporter, a benefactor of many.
How many ministries today would struggle without faithful women like Phoebe?

- ✓ Women who organize church events, making sure everything runs smoothly.
- ✓ Women who handle church finances with integrity.
- ✓ Women who care for the sick, visit the elderly, and intercede in prayer.
- ✓ Women who welcome strangers and create a loving environment for worship.

Phoebe reminds us that every act of service matters.

Old Testament Example: Deborah – A Leader Who Served with Wisdom

Phoebe was not the first woman to serve in leadership. The Old Testament also gives us remarkable examples, including Deborah.
Deborah was a prophetess, a judge, and a wise leader in Israel (Judges 4-5).
People came from all over seeking her counsel. But she did more than just offer wisdom—she led Israel to victory against their enemies.
Her story proves that servant leadership is not passive—it is powerful.
Just as Phoebe served by supporting the church and aiding Paul, Deborah served by providing wisdom and leading God's people to victory.
Both women remind us that serving with excellence leads to great impact.

Real-Life Example: Women Excelling in Church Administration and Service

I once met a woman named Margaret, who had served in her church for over 30 years.

She never stood behind a pulpit. She never preached a sermon. But her faithfulness and diligence kept the church running.

Margaret:

- ✓ Organized finances, making sure missionaries were supported.
- ✓ Coordinated outreach events, bringing people to Christ.
- ✓ Mentored young women, teaching them to serve with excellence.

She was the Phoebe of her generation—and because of her work, her church flourished.

This is the beauty of serving.

It is not about being seen—it is about making a lasting impact.

Final Encouragement: Serve with Excellence

Phoebe's name may only appear once in scripture, but her legacy echoes through time.

She was faithful in her role.

She was honored by Paul.

She was trusted with a great responsibility.

God still calls people like Phoebe today—people who serve with joy, diligence, and excellence.

No act of service is too small. No contribution goes unnoticed by God.

Jesus Himself came to serve—and when we serve with excellence, we reflect His heart to the world.

Will you be a Phoebe in your generation?

Reflection Questions

1. *What does Phoebe's life teach us about serving with excellence in the church?*

2. *In what areas of ministry have you been called to serve? How can you do it with greater excellence?*
3. *Who are the "Phoebes" in your church or community—those who serve faithfully behind the scenes? How can you honor and support them?*
4. *How does Deborah's leadership in the Old Testament inspire you to serve with courage and wisdom?*
5. *Jesus said, "Whoever wants to become great among you must be your servant." (Matthew 20:26) How can you apply this truth to your life today?*

No matter how small or great your role in the Kingdom may seem, serve with excellence, like Phoebe.
Because in the eyes of God—servants are the greatest of all.

Lydia – A Businesswoman with a Heart for God

When we think of influential figures in the early church, our minds often go to apostles, preachers, and missionaries. But what about business leaders? What about those who fund the gospel, open their homes, and use their influence to expand the Kingdom of God?

Enter Lydia—a woman of both wealth and deep faith. She was not just another convert; she was the first recorded believer in Europe and a pioneer in using business as a ministry platform.

She was a merchant of purple cloth—a rare and luxurious product worn by royalty and the wealthy. Yet despite her financial success, her heart remained open to the things of God.

Her story is one of balance—between business and faith, between wealth and worship, between industry and intimacy with God.

And she teaches us that our careers and resources, when surrendered to God, can become powerful tools for His Kingdom.

A Divine Appointment by the River

Lydia's story begins in Acts 16:14-15, where she is introduced as:

"A seller of purple, from the city of Thyatira, who worshiped God. The Lord opened her heart to heed the things spoken by Paul. And when she and her household were baptized, she begged us, saying, 'If you have judged me to be faithful to the Lord, come to my house and stay.' So she persuaded us."

This was no ordinary encounter.

Paul and his missionary team had not originally planned to visit Philippi—they had been led there through a vision from God (Acts 16:9-10).
When they arrived, they did not find a synagogue (indicating a lack of Jewish presence). Instead, they found a group of women gathered by the river in prayer.
Lydia was among them.
This moment reveals something extraordinary:

- ✓ Lydia was already a worshiper of God. Though she may not have fully understood the gospel yet, her heart was inclined toward the Lord.
- ✓ She was open to truth. Scripture says that "the Lord opened her heart"—showing that true transformation happens when we are receptive to God's voice.
- ✓ Her faith led to action. Immediately after her conversion, she and her entire household were baptized.

And then she did something remarkable—she invited Paul and his team into her home.
This was no small act. By opening her home, she created a place where the gospel could take root in Philippi.

Using Resources for the Gospel

Lydia's wealth is important to consider—not because it made her superior, but because she used it for God's purposes.
She was a merchant of purple cloth, a product associated with royalty and high status. This means:

- ✓ She was financially successful. Purple dye was expensive, and only the wealthy could afford it. Lydia's business must have been thriving.

- ✓ She was influential. She likely had connections with high-ranking officials and affluent members of society.
- ✓ She was independent. Unlike many women of her time, she controlled her own finances and made her own decisions.

But here's what makes Lydia truly special:

She did not let her wealth control her—she used it to serve God.

- ✓ She immediately offered her home to Paul and his companions, making it a center for ministry.
- ✓ She likely helped support Paul's work financially (as he later wrote about the generosity of the Philippian church).
- ✓ Her house became the first church in Philippi—a place where believers could gather, pray, and be discipled.

Lydia understood something that many struggle with today:

Money is not evil—but how we use it matters.

Balancing Faith and Financial Success

There is often a tension between faith and financial success. Some believe that wealth and spirituality cannot coexist. Others fall into the trap of chasing riches at the cost of their faith.

Lydia found the balance.

She was prosperous but not greedy.

She was successful but not self-centered.

She was wealthy but generous.

Jesus taught this same principle when He said:

"Seek first the Kingdom of God and His righteousness, and all these things shall be added to you." (Matthew 6:33)

Lydia sought God first—and she used her business as a platform for ministry.

Old Testament Example: Abraham – Blessed to Be a Blessing

Lydia's story echoes an earlier biblical figure: Abraham.

God promised Abraham:

"I will bless you, and you shall be a blessing." (Genesis 12:2)

Abraham was extremely wealthy, possessing flocks, herds, silver, and gold (Genesis 13:2). But his wealth was not just for himself—it was meant to bless nations.

Just like Lydia, Abraham's resources became a tool for God's purposes.

Both Lydia and Abraham show us that God blesses His people—not so they can hoard wealth, but so they can be a blessing to others.

Real-Life Example: Women Using Business as a Platform for Ministry

Today, many women follow in Lydia's footsteps—combining business with faith to impact lives for Christ.

I once met a woman named Angela, who ran a successful clothing business. Like Lydia, she sold beautiful garments to high-end clients. But she saw her business as more than just a way to make money.

- ✓ She used her store as a ministry hub, hosting Bible studies for customers and employees.
- ✓ She mentored young women in business, teaching them to succeed with integrity.
- ✓ She donated a portion of her profits to fund mission work in unreached areas.

Angela was not just a businesswoman—she was a kingdom builder.

Like Lydia, she understood that business is not separate from faith—it is an extension of it.

Final Encouragement: Your Work Can Glorify God

Lydia's story teaches us that faith and financial success are not enemies—they can work together for God's glory.

She reminds us that:

- ✓ Business can be a ministry. Your workplace can be a mission field.
- ✓ Wealth is a tool, not a trap. If we use it wisely, it can bless many.
- ✓ An open heart leads to open hands. When we surrender our lives to God, He will use us in extraordinary ways.

Lydia was not just a merchant—she was a minister.

And so are you.

No matter what your job is—whether you're a business owner, a teacher, an artist, or a stay-at-home parent—your work can serve God.

Will you use your resources for the Kingdom like Lydia did?

Reflection Questions

1. *How did Lydia's business success help advance the gospel, and how can your work do the same?*
2. *Do you see your career or business as a ministry? Why or why not?*
3. *What are some practical ways you can use your financial resources to bless others?*
4. *In what ways does Lydia's story challenge your perspective on wealth and faith?*

5. *Abraham was "blessed to be a blessing." How can you apply this principle in your own life?*

Lydia’s life was a testament to faith in action—a woman who used her resources wisely and allowed God to work through her success.
May we all follow her example—seeking God first and using what we have for His glory.

Priscilla – Partnership in Ministry

The story of Priscilla is one of partnership, purpose, and power in the Kingdom of God. She and her husband, Aquila, were an extraordinary couple—one of the earliest ministry teams in the New Testament, working side by side to teach, disciple, and strengthen the church.

In a time when women were often expected to take a backseat in religious matters, Priscilla stood out—not as a silent supporter, but as an active teacher, mentor, and leader.

She was not merely Aquila's wife—she was his partner in ministry, equally engaged in spreading the gospel and equipping others for the work of God.

Priscilla's life challenges traditional expectations and reminds us that God calls both men and women to work together for His purposes.

A Powerful Ministry Team

Priscilla and Aquila's story unfolds in Acts 18, where we first meet them as Jewish tentmakers living in Corinth. They had been expelled from Rome under the decree of Emperor Claudius and were making a new life in Greece.

It was here that they encountered Paul, who was also a tentmaker by trade.

Scripture tells us:

"After these things Paul departed from Athens and went to Corinth. And he found a certain Jew named Aquila, born in Pontus, who had recently come from Italy with his wife Priscilla (because Claudius had commanded all the Jews to depart from Rome); and he came to them. So, because he was of the same

trade, he stayed with them and worked; for by occupation they were tentmakers." (Acts 18:1-3)

What began as a business connection quickly turned into a spiritual partnership.

Priscilla and Aquila opened their home to Paul, providing hospitality, support, and friendship. But their involvement did not stop at tentmaking—they became some of Paul's closest ministry companions.

Later, when Paul left Corinth, they traveled with him to Ephesus, where they remained to help establish and strengthen the church there.

Priscilla was not behind the scenes—she was on the front lines, serving alongside her husband in a powerful, effective way.

Discipling and Teaching Together

One of the most remarkable moments in Priscilla's ministry is found in Acts 18:24-26, when she and Aquila encountered Apollos, a gifted preacher who was passionate but incomplete in his understanding of the gospel.

"Now a certain Jew named Apollos, born at Alexandria, an eloquent man and mighty in the Scriptures, came to Ephesus. This man had been instructed in the way of the Lord; and being fervent in spirit, he spoke and taught accurately the things of the Lord, though he knew only the baptism of John. So he began to speak boldly in the synagogue. When Aquila and Priscilla heard him, they took him aside and explained to him the way of God more accurately." (Acts 18:24-26)

This moment is significant for several reasons:

- ✓ Apollos was already a gifted speaker—but he was lacking full understanding.

- ✓ Priscilla and Aquila did not criticize him publicly—they corrected and discipled him in private, showing wisdom and grace.
- ✓ Both Priscilla and Aquila were involved in teaching him—this was not Aquila leading while Priscilla listened in the background.

In fact, in many places where this couple is mentioned, Priscilla's name is listed first (Acts 18:26; Romans 16:3; 2 Timothy 4:19), suggesting that she was a prominent teacher and leader.

Priscilla's role in mentoring Apollos reminds us that ministry is not about status or titles—it is about faithfully equipping others in the truth.

She and Aquila were not apostles, pastors, or prophets, yet they were powerful influencers in the early church.

The Power of Teamwork in Advancing the Kingdom

Priscilla and Aquila demonstrate that marriage is not just about companionship—it can be a powerful tool for ministry.

Their relationship was one of partnership—where each person's gifts were recognized and used for the advancement of the gospel.

They worked together in business, in hospitality, in teaching, and in discipleship.

Their home became a place of refuge for believers, a meeting space for the church, and a launching pad for missionaries.

In Romans 16:3-4, Paul acknowledges their great impact, writing:

"Greet Priscilla and Aquila, my fellow workers in Christ Jesus, who risked their own necks for my life, to whom not only I give thanks, but also all the churches of the Gentiles."

This tells us something crucial:

- ✓ They were not just casual believers. They were deeply committed, even willing to risk their lives for the gospel.
- ✓ They had an influence far beyond their local church. Paul says that all the churches of the Gentiles owed them gratitude.
- ✓ They were equally engaged in ministry. Priscilla is named alongside Aquila as a "fellow worker"—not a helper or assistant, but a co-laborer in Christ.

Their story challenges traditional ideas of ministry and proves that God calls both men and women to work together for His purposes.

Old Testament Example: Deborah and Barak

Priscilla's role as a leader alongside her husband is echoed in the Old Testament through Deborah and Barak (Judges 4-5).

Deborah was a prophetess and judge of Israel—a woman of wisdom, courage, and leadership.

When Israel faced oppression from the Canaanites, Deborah summoned Barak and commanded him to lead the army against their enemies.

Barak hesitated, saying:

"If you will go with me, then I will go; but if you will not go with me, I will not go." (Judges 4:8)

Deborah agreed to go, but she made it clear that victory would come through a woman, not through Barak.

Their partnership led to a great triumph for Israel, proving that when men and women work together in God's plan, victory is assured.

Just as Deborah and Barak fought side by side for Israel, Priscilla and Aquila labored side by side for the gospel.

Real-Life Example: Couples Serving in Ministry Together

I once met a couple, David and Sarah, who planted a church in a small town. David was the main preacher, but Sarah was deeply involved in counseling, mentoring young women, and leading Bible studies.

Their home was always open to those in need.

Together, they created an environment where people felt welcomed, discipled, and strengthened in their faith.

Like Priscilla and Aquila, they served as a team—complementing each other's strengths and weaknesses, building the Kingdom side by side.

Final Encouragement: Answering the Call Together

Priscilla's story reminds us that:

- ✓ Ministry is a team effort. Whether in marriage, friendships, or church partnerships, we are stronger together.
- ✓ Women have an important role in teaching and discipleship. Priscilla was not limited by cultural expectations—she stepped into her calling with boldness.
- ✓ Hospitality and mentorship are powerful tools for the gospel. A simple act of opening your home can change lives.

God is still calling Priscillas and Aquilas today—people willing to work together, teach truth, and serve with devotion.

Will you answer that call?

Reflection Questions

1. *How does Priscilla's ministry challenge traditional views on women in leadership?*

2. *What strengths do you bring to ministry, and how can you work with others to maximize impact?*
3. *How can your home or workplace become a space for discipleship and hospitality?*
4. *Are there areas where you need to step out in boldness, like Priscilla did?*
5. *How can you support or partner with others in advancing the Kingdom of God?*

May we all learn from Priscilla's courage, wisdom, and willingness to serve.

Lois & Eunice – Generational Faithfulness

There is something powerful about a legacy of faith. Some people inherit great wealth, family businesses, or valuable properties, but the greatest inheritance any child can receive is a foundation of faith. This is what young Timothy received—not from a father who was spiritually strong, but from two remarkable women: his grandmother Lois and his mother Eunice. Their influence was so profound that even the great apostle Paul took notice. In his letter to Timothy, Paul wrote:

"I am reminded of your sincere faith, which first lived in your grandmother Lois and in your mother Eunice and, I am persuaded, now lives in you also." (2 Timothy 1:5, NIV)

This one verse speaks volumes. It tells us that faith is not always taught in grand theological institutions or learned from renowned preachers. Sometimes, it is passed down in the quiet, everyday moments of life—through a praying mother, a wise grandmother, or a godly home.

Lois and Eunice may not have been apostles, prophets, or leaders of synagogues, but they shaped a leader who would impact the early church and generations beyond. Their story is a reminder that faithful parenting and godly influence can raise up men and women who change the world.

Shaping a Leader Through Faith

Timothy is first introduced in Acts 16:1, where we learn that he was the son of a Jewish mother who was a believer and a Greek father. While little is said about his father, it is clear that his spiritual formation came not from his paternal lineage, but from the women in his life.

Paul, a man known for mentoring and discipling future leaders, immediately recognized Timothy's potential. He took Timothy under his wing, and together, they traveled on missionary journeys, planting churches and strengthening believers. Timothy later became a pastor in Ephesus, a trusted leader, and a key figure in the growth of the early church.

But before Paul ever poured into Timothy, Lois and Eunice had already done the groundwork. They were the ones who instilled faith, nurtured his understanding of scripture, and set the example of godliness.

Paul himself acknowledges this when he writes to Timothy:

"But as for you, continue in what you have learned and have become convinced of, because you know those from whom you learned it, and how from infancy you have known the Holy Scriptures, which are able to make you wise for salvation through faith in Christ Jesus." (2 Timothy 3:14-15, NIV)

This tells us two things:

- ✓ Timothy had been taught the scriptures from infancy. Lois and Eunice did not wait until he was older; they began sowing the seeds of faith in his heart when he was just a child.
- ✓ Their teaching was more than just words—it was a lived example. Paul reminds Timothy that he learned from people he could trust. Their faith was real, sincere, and evident in their daily lives.

This is the essence of generational faithfulness. It is not just about telling children what to believe—it is about living a life that inspires them to believe.

The Power of Faith Passed Down Through Generations

The story of Lois and Eunice is not the first time we see faith passed down through generations. Throughout the Bible, we find examples of godly parents and grandparents shaping the destiny of their children through their influence.

One of the clearest examples is Abraham, Isaac, and Jacob.

God made a covenant with Abraham, promising to make him the father of many nations. This covenant did not end with Abraham—it was passed down to Isaac, then to Jacob, and eventually to the entire nation of Israel.

In Genesis 18:19, God says of Abraham:

"For I have chosen him, so that he will direct his children and his household after him to keep the way of the Lord by doing what is right and just, so that the Lord will bring about for Abraham what he has promised him."

Abraham's responsibility was not just to receive the blessing but to pass down the knowledge of God to the next generation.

Similarly, King David instilled faith in his son Solomon by teaching him the importance of following God. In 1 Chronicles 28:9, David tells Solomon:

"And you, my son Solomon, acknowledge the God of your father, and serve him with wholehearted devotion and with a willing mind, for the Lord searches every heart and understands every desire and every thought."

The impact of godly parenting echoes through generations—just as it did with Lois and Eunice. Their faithfulness did not just affect Timothy's life; it influenced the entire church through his leadership.

Real-Life Example: Women Raising Godly Children

I once met a woman named Margaret, who raised four children as a single mother. Life was difficult—she worked long hours, struggled to make ends meet, and often wondered if she was making any real impact.

But every night, without fail, she gathered her children for prayer. She spoke scriptures over them, taught them to trust in God, and led by example.

Years later, her eldest son became a pastor, one daughter became a missionary, and her youngest son became a Bible teacher.

One day, when asked how she managed to raise such godly children, she simply smiled and said:

"I just did what my mother did for me. I planted the seeds, and God made them grow."

This is the power of generational faithfulness.

It is not always about having a perfect life or a perfect family. It is about being faithful with what God has given you—pouring into the next generation with love, wisdom, and the Word of God.

Final Encouragement: The Influence of a Godly Home

If you are a parent, a grandparent, or even a mentor to younger believers, your role in shaping the next generation is invaluable.

Lois and Eunice did not have high positions in the church. They were not apostles or prophets. But their faith changed the course of history by raising up

Timothy, who went on to strengthen the church and spread the gospel.

You may never know the full impact of your faithfulness—but rest assured, God is using you to shape lives for His glory.

Whether you are a mother raising children, a teacher mentoring students, or a grandparent speaking life into your family, your faith matters.

You are part of a legacy that will outlive you.

So, like Lois and Eunice, remain steadfast. Keep teaching. Keep praying. Keep leading by example.

Your influence may just be the spark that ignites a future leader in the Kingdom of God.

Reflection Questions

1. *Who has played a significant role in shaping your faith? How did their example impact you?*
2. *Are you intentionally passing down faith to the next generation? In what ways can you do this more effectively?*
3. *How can you create a home environment where faith is nurtured and strengthened?*
4. *Have you ever felt like your efforts in teaching or mentoring were unnoticed? How does the story of Lois and Eunice encourage you?*
5. *What small, consistent steps can you take to ensure that faith continues beyond your lifetime?*

May God bless you as you walk in generational faithfulness, planting seeds that will bear fruit for generations to come.

Bonus Chapter: Praying Mothers – Women Who Shaped Destiny Through Prayer

There is nothing more powerful than a mother's prayer. Throughout history, kingdoms have risen and fallen, wars have been won and lost, and great leaders have emerged—but behind many of these moments stood a praying mother.

A mother's prayer is not just a whispered request in the darkness; it is a battle cry, a declaration of faith, and a seed planted in the heart of a child. Some of the greatest men in the Bible—prophets, judges, apostles, and church leaders—were shaped by the faithfulness of their mothers.

These women were not always highly esteemed by society, nor did they always have ideal circumstances, but they prayed, believed, and refused to give up. Their persistence shaped the destiny of their children, and through them, the Kingdom of God was advanced.

Let us take a journey through scripture and meet some of these extraordinary mothers—women whose faith moved heaven and changed the world.

Jochebed – The Mother Who Trusted God With Her Son (Exodus 2:1-10, Hebrews 11:23)

Jochebed's story is one of desperate faith in desperate times. The Israelites were suffering under the cruel oppression of Pharaoh, who had issued a decree that every Hebrew baby boy must be thrown into the Nile River.

Imagine the anguish in Jochebed's heart when she discovered she was pregnant. She did not know whether she was carrying a boy or a girl, but she did know the fate that awaited her child if it was a son.

When Moses was born, she saw that he was no ordinary child. She refused to let Pharaoh's command dictate his destiny. For three months, she hid her baby, nursing him in secret, knowing that at any moment, soldiers could come and take him away.

But her faith was greater than her fear.

Unable to hide him any longer, she placed him in a basket and set him afloat on the very river that was meant to bring his death. But she did not abandon him. She entrusted him to the hands of God.

God honored Jochebed's faith. Pharaoh's own daughter found Moses and unknowingly paid Jochebed to nurse her own son. Moses grew up in the palace, educated in the wisdom of Egypt, yet his heart remained with his people.

Because of his mother's faith, Moses became the deliverer of Israel.

Her story teaches us the power of surrendering our children to God. Sometimes, we cannot control what happens to them, but we can trust the One who holds their future.

Hannah – The Mother Who Prayed for a Son and Gave Him Back to God (1 Samuel 1:1-28)

Hannah's story is one of agonizing prayer and divine faithfulness. She was barren, and in ancient Israel, this was considered a disgrace. Year after year, she endured ridicule, but she refused to accept her situation as final.

One day, she went to the temple and poured out her soul before God.

"In her deep anguish Hannah prayed to the Lord, weeping bitterly." (1 Samuel 1:10)

She made a vow: If God gave her a son, she would dedicate him to the Lord all the days of his life.

God heard her prayer, and Samuel was born. True to her word, Hannah brought him to the temple as a young child and gave him to Eli, the priest, so that he could serve the Lord.

Samuel grew up to be one of Israel's greatest prophets, a man who anointed kings and led the nation back to God.

Hannah's story reminds us that when we dedicate our children to the Lord, He will use them for His purposes.

The Mother and Grandmother of Timothy – Passing Down Faith (2 Timothy 1:5, 3:14-15)

Timothy did not grow up with a spiritually strong father. His father was Greek, likely an unbeliever. But Timothy's mother, Eunice, and grandmother, Lois, made sure that did not hinder him from knowing God. They taught him the Scriptures from infancy, filling his heart with the Word of God.

Paul later wrote to Timothy:

"I am reminded of your sincere faith, which first lived in your grandmother Lois and in your mother Eunice and, I am persuaded, now lives in you also." (2 Timothy 1:5)

Because of their influence, Timothy became a key leader in the early church, pastoring in Ephesus and working alongside Paul.

Their story shows us that even in homes where fathers are absent or spiritually disengaged, a praying mother and grandmother can shape a leader for the Kingdom.

Elizabeth – The Mother Who Bore a Forerunner (Luke 1:5-25, 57-66)

Elizabeth was barren for many years, but God had a plan beyond what she could imagine.

In her old age, she conceived John the Baptist, the prophet who would prepare the way for Jesus.

Elizabeth's faith was evident in how she rejoiced over God's promise and recognized the divine calling upon her son's life. When Mary, pregnant with Jesus, visited her, Elizabeth was filled with the Holy Spirit and declared,

"Blessed are you among women, and blessed is the child you will bear!" (Luke 1:42)

Her story teaches us that God's timing is perfect, and He can use mothers at any stage of life to raise children for His purpose.

Mary – The Mother Who Surrendered to God's Will (Luke 1:26-38, John 19:25-27)

No mother in history carried a greater responsibility than Mary. She was chosen to be the mother of Jesus, the Messiah, the Son of God.

Mary's heart must have been filled with wonder and fear when the angel Gabriel appeared to her. Yet, she humbly accepted God's will:

"I am the Lord's servant. May your word to me be fulfilled." (Luke 1:38)

She nurtured Jesus, raised Him in wisdom and grace, and eventually stood at the foot of the cross, watching her son give His life for the salvation of the world.

Mary's story is a testament to the cost of saying "yes" to God, even when it is difficult.

Final Encouragement: The Power of a Mother's Prayer

Every mother in this chapter prayed, believed, and surrendered their children to God. Some, like Hannah and Jochebed, had to let their sons go.

Others, like Lois, Eunice, and Mary, stayed by their side and nurtured them into greatness.
But none of their prayers were wasted.
Your prayers are powerful. They shape the future, move heaven, and can lead your children into their divine destiny.

Reflection Questions

1. *Which mother's story impacted you the most? Why?*
2. *How has your own mother or grandmother's faith shaped your life?*
3. *Are you consistently praying over your children, spiritual children, or the next generation?*
4. *What steps can you take to ensure your faith is passed down to those who come after you?*
5. *Is there an area in your child's life where you need to trust God more? How can you surrender it to Him today?*

May God bless you as you stand in the gap and pray for the next generation. Your prayers will not return void.

Conclusion: Embracing the Pillars of Womanhood

As we journey through the pages of history, exploring the lives of remarkable women in Scripture, one thing becomes overwhelmingly clear: God has always used women as pillars in His divine plan. Each woman we have studied stands as a beacon of faith, courage, perseverance, and devotion, illuminating a path that all of us, regardless of our circumstances, can follow.

Recap of Key Lessons from Each Woman

Miriam taught us the dangers of jealousy and the responsibility of a worshipper. A leader in song and dance, yet she allowed pride to taint her role, reminding us that humility must accompany our calling (Exodus 15:20-21, Numbers 12:1-15).

Mary, the mother of Jesus, demonstrated the ultimate surrender to God's will. In saying "yes" to the angel's announcement, she showed us what it means to trust God's plan, even when it doesn't make sense (Luke 1:26-38).

Elizabeth exemplified faithfulness in the waiting. Her story proves that God's promises are not void just because they are delayed. Through her, we learn that His timing is perfect (Luke 1:5-25, 57-66).

Mary Magdalene embodied devotion that transforms. Freed from bondage, she became the first witness of the Resurrection, proving that those who have been forgiven much, love much (Luke 8:1-3, John 20:11-18).

The woman with the issue of blood displayed a faith that pushes through. Her desperation led her to reach for Jesus, and in doing so, she found healing, reinforcing the necessity of persistent faith (Mark 5:25-34).

The Samaritan woman showed us how evangelism through personal testimony can spark revival. Once an outcast, she became a mouthpiece for the Messiah, proving that God restores identity and purpose (John 4:1-42).

The persistent widow taught us the power of unyielding prayer. Through her example, we learn that persistence in intercession moves the heart of God (Luke 18:1-8).

Phoebe demonstrated how serving with excellence in the Church can elevate the work of the Gospel. As a deacon, she played a crucial role in ministry, proving that every role in the Church matters (Romans 16:1-2).

Lydia, a businesswoman, showed us the beauty of balancing faith and financial success. She used her resources for the Gospel, proving that business can be a platform for ministry (Acts 16:14-15, 40).

Priscilla exemplified the power of partnership in ministry. Alongside her husband, she discipled others, showing that teamwork advances the Kingdom (Acts 18:24-26).

Lois and Eunice illustrated the impact of generational faithfulness. Their commitment to raising Timothy in the ways of the Lord proves that a mother and grandmother's faith can shape a future leader (2 Timothy 1:5).

Encouragement to Step into Divine Purpose

Every woman in this book had a choice—to step into God's calling or shrink back. None of them were without struggle, pain, or challenges. Some faced rejection, others battled personal weaknesses, and some had to navigate long seasons of waiting. Yet, in the end, each one chose to trust God. And because of their obedience, they left a legacy that continues to impact lives today.

Women today are called to do the same. You may feel unseen, insignificant, or unqualified, but let the lives of these women remind you that God does not call the perfect—He perfects those He calls. Your surrender, faith, and persistence can shape the generations that come after you. Whether in your home, your church, your workplace, or your community, God is looking for women who will say, "Here I am, Lord. Use me."

A Call to Rise as Pillars in Homes, Churches, and Societies

In a world that constantly redefines womanhood, we must return to the Biblical foundation of what it truly means to be a woman of God. We are called to be strong yet humble, bold yet gracious, persistent in faith yet surrendered to God's timing. We are to be warriors in prayer, builders of faith, and nurturers of the next generation.

God is calling women today to rise up—

- ✓ *To be like Miriam and lead others in worship while guarding against pride.*
- ✓ *To be like Mary and say "yes" to God's plan, no matter the cost.*
- ✓ *To be like Elizabeth and remain faithful in the waiting.*
- ✓ *To be like Mary Magdalene and walk in the transforming power of Christ.*
- ✓ *To be like the woman with the issue of blood and push through in faith.*

- ✓ *To be like the Samaritan woman and share our testimonies boldly.*
- ✓ *To be like the persistent widow and never cease interceding.*
- ✓ *To be like Phoebe and serve the Church with excellence.*
- ✓ *To be like Lydia and use our resources for the Gospel.*
- ✓ *To be like Priscilla and support our spouses in ministry.*
- ✓ *To be like Lois and Eunice and raise godly children who will change the world.*

This is the time to embrace our divine calling and stand firm as pillars of faith in our homes, churches, and societies. Let us not wait for ideal conditions, for a more convenient season, or for someone else to take the lead. The time is now.

Reflection Questions

1. *Which woman's story resonated with you the most? Why?*
2. *In what areas of your life do you need to trust God's plan more?*
3. *How can you use your personal testimony to encourage others?*
4. *Are you persistent in prayer, or do you give up too easily? How can you grow in this area?*
5. *How can you use your resources, time, and talents to further God's Kingdom?*

May this book inspire you to walk boldly in your divine purpose, knowing that you are called, chosen, and deeply loved by God. Rise up, woman of faith, and take your place in His grand story!

About the Author 'GERARD ASSEY'

Gerard Assey is a Graduate in Economics, a PGD in Management (HRD) and holds a Doctorate in Leadership. Gerard holds several International Qualifications in Sales, Debt Collection, Training & Teaching, and is a 'Fellow' of the prestigious 'Institute of Sales & Marketing Management'-UK, a Certified NLP Practitioner, a 'Certified Trainer', an 'Accredited Management Teacher-Behavioral Sciences', a 'Certified Competency Facilitator', a 'Certified Management Consultant'- (the International credentials of a professional management consultant, awarded in accordance with global standards of the ICMCI); and a Certification from the University of Michigan in 'Successful Negotiation: Essential Strategies and Skills'

He is also a Member of the 'National Association of Sales Professionals' backed with several years experience in varied industries, both in India and Overseas. He also holds an 'Etiquette Consultant' Certification from the USA (by Sue Fox, Author of Best Seller: 'Business Etiquette for Dummies'. She has trained some of the top celebrities' world over). He was also a recipient of a scholarship for extensive training in Japan on 'Corporate Management for India'.

Gerard Assey is 'Founder & Chief Corporate Trainer' of the Group: **'Citius, Altius, Fortius Unlimited'**- an organization that **celebrated 20 years of Glorious Service** in 2021, focusing on 3 Core Competencies:

People. Performance. Profit; in functional areas of Sales & Marketing, HR & Organizational Development, covering Recruitment, Training & Consultancy!

Having managed organizations with large Sales Forces in India & Overseas, his specialization cover extensive areas of Sales Training (All levels - Presentation, Negotiation, Key/ Strategic Accounts Management & Managerial Skills for all sectors), Bid Proposal/ Capture Planning/ Management Trainings, Retail Sales, Customer Service & Customer Retention Programs, Training for Prevention & Collection of Debt, Self & Personal Development Programs (Time Management, Teamwork & Team Building, Business Etiquette & Personal Grooming, Leadership & Managerial Skills, People Management Skills, Train-the-Trainer etc), including preparation of Custom-designed Business Manuals for Internal (HR, Induction, and Sales etc) & External use (Instruction, User Manuals).

Gerard has successfully conducted over 6440 Trainings & Workshops (as of Mar '25) all across India, Middle East, Africa, Europe & S.E. Asia. Besides public programs conducted regularly, both in India & Overseas, he has some of the top names as clients whom he services from Single Owners to large Public & Government undertakings, covering all sectors, for their in-house needs.

His website: www.CollectionSkills.com is the only one in this part of the world to be featured in the 'Collections & Credit Risk Magazine-USA' under 'Who's Who in Training' and ranks TOP, along with other websites listed below on most search engines.

Gerard is author of 177 books already (Mar 2025), all the books being available on all online platforms and outlets as E-books and Paperbacks

A few of our business related books:

1. Bite-sized Bits on Commonsense Management
2. Heart to Heart on Life's Principles'
3. How to become a Successful Manager
4. The Sales Professionals' Master Workbook of S.Y.S.T.E.M.S
5. The Professional Business Email Etiquette Handbook & Guide
6. The Professional Business Video-Conferencing Etiquette Handbook & Guide
7. Professional Presentation Skills
8. Exceptional Customer Service
9. Professional Tele-Marketing Skills
10. Professional Debt Collection Skills
11. The G.R.E.A.T. Sales & Service Workbook
12. Sales Training Advantage for Results (*The Ultimate Sales Training Manual to enable you stand out as a S.T.A.R.*)
13. CEO Daily Planner & Organizer
14. The Sales Professionals' Master Daily Planner
15. The Professional Debt Collector's Master Daily Planner
16. My Daily Planner & Organizer
17. MY EMERGENCY INFORMATION RECORD (Family Emergency & Peace of Mind Planner)
18. The Ultimate Therapist & Counselors Planner and Organizer
19. Building an Ethical Workplace
20. Managing Relationships at Work
21. Managing Business Meetings Effectively
22. Effective Delegation Skills
23. Goal Setting for Success
24. B2B Selling by Email
25. Professional Business Etiquette & Grooming
26. Dining Etiquette & Table Manners
27. Effective Networking Skills
28. Grooming, Etiquette & Manners for Teens, Young Adults & Future Leaders
29. Inter-Personal Skills
30. Get Ready, Get Hired!
31. Selling in a Recession

32. Effective Receivables Management in an Economic Downturn!
33. Real Estate & Property Sales Training
34. Credit Sales & Accounts Receivable Management
35. Selling Skills for Real Estate & Property Advisors
36. Take G.R.E.A.T. C.A.R.E!
37. Spa, Salon & Health Club Selling Skills
38. Selling Travel, Holiday & MICE Services
39. Selling Skills for Spa's, Salons & Health Clubs
40. Retailing in Salons & Spas
41. Selling Holiday, Vacation, Tours & Packages
42. The Power of Sales Referrals
43. Selling Luxury
44. Technical Selling Skills
45. Financial Advisors Sales Training
46. Dealing with Burnout at Work Monopolize Your Markets
47. Selling to Affluent Customers
48. Growing up with Grace
49. Financial Selling Skills
50. *The Effective Manager's Guide: Key Skills to Thrive*
51. From Aspiring to Inspiring: A Guide for New Managers on the Rise
52. The Power of Focus
53. Selling with Integrity: Sell Like Jesus The Perfect Role Model!
54. 31 Habits of Champions: Your 31-Day Journey to Greatness
55. Rejecting Grasshopper Talk: From Grasshopper to Giant-Killer-*Defeating Giants Daily!*
56. Navigate the AI-Powered Future of Bid & Proposals: Up-Skill to Stay Relevant with Alternative Career Paths & Opportunities
57. Hiring Sales Winners
58. Present with Impact
59. Success Unlocked: *Breaking Free from Habits that Hold You Back*
60. Complaints to Cheers, Feedback to Gold: Mastering Complaints Management
61. Thriving Together: *Cultivating Diversity, Equity, and Inclusion*
62. Coaching Skills for Sales Managers

63. Soaring to Success in Business & Leadership: Swifter, Higher, Stronger!
64. From Classroom to Podium: A Student's Guide to Powerful Public Speaking & Presentation Skills
65. Developing Self-Discipline
66. The CEO's 31-Day Power Plan: Unlocking Success through Essential Traits
67. Credibility Matters
68. A Winning Attitude
69. Bid & Proposal Management Using AI
70. Sales Forecasting: A Practical & Proven Guide to Strategic Sales Forecasting
71. Elevate & Energize: *50 Dynamic & Fun Activities for Peak Workplace Morale*
72. 'Sales SOS! Sales on Fire! *30 Days to Conquer Chaos & the Nightmares of Success!'*
73. Mastering Sales Managerial Skills: *Building High-Performing Teams & Driving Exceptional Results*
74. Eagle-Eyed Leadership: Unleashing the Power of 31 Lessons from Eagles
75. The Ultimate Employee Training Guide: *Training Today, Leading Tomorrow*
76. Being More Accountable at Work
77. Creating a Culture of Continuous Improvement
78. Effective Questioning & Listening Skills
79. The Power of Value Selling
80. The Growth Mindset
81. Mastering Professional Help Desk Skills
82. The Power to Lead with Empathy
83. Being Prepared: The Key to Unlocking Success
84. Youthful Spark-Youth Energizers, Activities and Games-Igniting the Fun in Youth
85. Ignite your Motivation for Success
86. Elevate Your Executive Presence: *Your Roadmap to Executive Excellence*
87. Smart Decisions: *Mastering Problem Solving with Strategic Solutions for Business Success*
88. Strategic Planning: *Developing and Implementing Strategic Plans to Achieve Long-Term Business Goals*
89. The Power of Stay Interviews
90. Developing G.R.I.T.
91. Adaptability

92. Diagnosis- *A Key Skill for Leadership*
93. The Burnout-Proof Salesperson: *The Master Guide to Preventing Stress & Burnout*- Strategies for Thriving in Sales
94. Learning from Failure: *Keys to Success*
95. Customer Success Management
96. Overcoming the Killers of Motivation
97. The C-Suite Code: *Mastering Skills for Executive Excellence'*
98. Dealing with Difficult Customers
99. Unlocking Your Potential: Mastering the Top 20 Life Skills for a Brighter Future
100. Nurturing Tomorrow's Leaders: *Essential Soft Skills Every Child Must Learn*
101. Lively & Fun Party Games for Seniors & Elders
102. Role Playing for Sales Champions: From Practice to Performance
103. Fun and Exciting Party Games for Kids
104. Case Studies for Sales
105. Role-Playing for Unbeatable Customer Service
106. Case Studies in Customer Service
107. Case Studies in Winning Negotiations
108. Case Studies in Management & Leadership
109. Case Studies in Human Resources & Talent Management
110. CEO Success Blueprint: The Essential Toolkit for CEOs and C-Level Executives
111. The Salesperson's Self-Coaching Guide: *Master Your Own Self-Coaching Plan for Success*
112. Overcoming Procrastination: *Your Ultimate Guide to Stop Delaying and Start Living Your Best Life*
113. When True Colors Are Exposed: *The Journey to Unmasking Humanity*
114. Life-Changing Habits for Teens: Teen Success Blueprint for a Bright Future
115. Workplace Stress-Free: *Proven Strategies to Thrive at Work and Beyond*

From the Ministry side, Gerard graduated in the very first batch of Charis Bible College-India & had for over 9 years served as a Part-time Faculty at Charis Bible College-Chennai (Andrew Wommack Ministries-Colorado, USA).
He is also a graduate of the Advanced Mentorship Program (AMP) and the Circle Of Ministerial Engagement (C.O.M.E.) of Prophet Jerome Fernando and a Spiritual Son of the Esteemed Prophet.
An accomplished author of several Secular & Christian Books, Gerard has been on the board of a few international organizations and boasts of being the SON of the MOST HIGH GOD: An ordinary guy following an extraordinary GOD!

...And some of his most recent Christian Books being:

1. A Bouquet of Praises for My KING
2. Christian Jokes for the Serious Religious' Folks!
3. Jesus Healed You!
4. Praise24Ever! (also in Tamil version)
5. The 5G Network of GOD
6. Building Faith over F.E.A.R- FACE EVERYTHING AND RISE with JESUS
7. Hebrew and Greek Praise and Worship Words
8. Godly Mothers' and Grandmothers' Bible Story time for Kids!
9. Miracles of Jesus in Pictures
10. Raise your Praise all 365 Days
11. Thanking GOD with an Attitude of Gratitude
12. Meditating on the Attributes of GOD
13. Puppet Scripts
14. Alcohol Ruins, JESUS Reforms, Renews & Restores!
15. Habakkuk 2:2 Christian Daily Journal, Planner & Organizer
16. ABC of GOD's Word for Handwriting Practice
17. Daily Bible Verse Handwriting Practice (Building Godly Character & Faith through Cursive Handwriting Practice!)
18. Guiding Light: Fun & Faith-Building Bible Activities for Children
19. Rejecting Grasshopper Talk: From Grasshopper to Giant-Killer-*Defeating Giants Daily!*
20. Teen Titans of Faith: *Building Courage, Determination & Christ-like-Esteem*
21. I AM Empowered: *Unleashing Divine Power with Positive Declarations*
22. Be A Solution Provider-*From Passion to Purpose*: *A Biblical Guide to Being the Answer to the World!*
23. Miracles of JESUS

24. Parables of Jesus for a Meaningful Life!
25. A Grateful Heart: Importance of Sharing Testimonies of GOD's Grace
26. Melodies of Worship to JESUS: 31 Songs of Praise & Worship From My Heart to HIS!
27. I AM SO BLESSED!
28. My Daily Cup of Energizer
29. 31 Leadership Lessons *from* Jesus- *The Supreme Leader*
30. Peace Amidst Storms: A Biblical Guide to Conquering S.T.R.E.S.S.
31. Rise Above: 20 Biblical Eagle Lessons for Life's Triumphs
32. Godly Goal Setting: *The FAITHFUL Blueprint for a Purpose-Driven Life*
33. The Profound Attributes of our Mighty GOD: Understanding the 10S's of the Almighty
34. Worship Now, Worship Forever: *A Journey from Earthly Praise to Eternal Glory*
35. Unceasing Praise & Worship: *365 Days to Worship the King*
36. The ROAR Within: *Living with Purpose and Authority through the Power of the Holy Spirit*
37. From Potential to Purpose: Unlocking and Multiplying Your Talents & Gifts for Kingdom Impact
38. Songs from the Heart: *Worshipping GOD in Your Own Tune & Melody*
39. Awakening Praise & Worship: Hebrew & Greek Words to Raise Your Praise
40. Sing a NEW Song to the LORD Everyday: *Daily Devotions of Praise & Worship to Lift Your Heart & Glorify HIS Name*
41. *The* A.R.O.M.A. of True Worship: *Creating Worship That Delights God*
42. Becoming A Kingdom Champion: *Embracing God's Call for a Life of Purpose & Victory*
43. The Busy Businessman's Daily Devotional: 366 Crisp Truths to Start Your Day Strong
44. The Teacher's Heart: *Daily Devotions for Educators*
45. Anchored! *A 31-Day Devotional for Students Facing Life's Challenges*
46. Suddenly! Unlocking Unorthodox Breakthroughs through Unusual Worship
47. Overcoming Adversity: *Lessons from the Bible for Modern Challenges*
48. LORD, Don't do it without me
49. Kingdom Leadership: *Biblical Principles for Modern Leaders*
50. Heartprints of God- *Growing God's Way:* Daily Devotions for Kids

to Shine Bright

51. Send Judah First: Let your Praises Go up First to See the Mighty Move of GOD
52. DIVINE MOMENTS: *Recognizing, Embracing, Preparing, and Walking into Life-Changing Encounters with God*
53. Be a Builder in the Kingdom: *The C.E.M.E.N.T. Guide to Creating a Lasting Legacy*
54. Unshakable: *Pillars of Godly Womanhood* (Pillars of Faith That Changed History)

Besides regularly contributing to business & trade journals, including international ones such as the 'Creative Training Techniques' and the 'Sales News' of the U.S.A, He is also a member of several prestigious bodies & trade associations, having participated in many Conferences & Workshops in India & Overseas.
Prior to his last assignment of leading & managing a large MNC as head, Gerard had a 3-year stint in the Middle East as a Consultant with a leading British Consultancy Firm.

As the past 'Official Country Representative' for the International Business Award- 'THE STEVIES'-(the business world's own Oscar) for about 4 years- he ensured a few Indian companies that qualify for the same every year!

Gerard can be contacted at:
Email: training@Sales-Training.in,training@CollectionSkills.com
Websites:

www.Sales-Training.in
www.EtiquetteWorks.in
www.CollectionSkills.com
www.RetailSalesTraining.in
www.SalesTrainingIndia.com
www.ManualPreparation.com
www.TrainingWithPuppets.com
www.FirstContactAcademy.com
www.SalesAndMarketingRecruiter.com

Our TRAININGS that can help your team

- ✓ **Sales Effectiveness**: Selling Skills for any Sector: Service/ Logistics/ FMCG Realty/ Insurance & Finance/ Media/ SPA's, Health Clubs & Salons/ Key Account Management, Effective Negotiation Skills/ Bid & Proposal Management Skills/ Retail Sales Training: Any Sector (Auto, Jewelry, Clothing, Luxury etc)
- ✓ **Customer Service Skills**-Complaints Handling & Customer Retention
- ✓ **Debt Prevention & Collection Skills**
- ✓ **Etiquette & Grooming**
- ✓ **Leadership & Managerial Skills**
- ✓ **Self & Personal Development Skills**: Presentation Skills/ Effective Communication Skills/Business Proposal Writing Skills/ Problem Solving & Decision Making Skills/ Empowering Secretaries-The perfect PA! (For Secretaries & PA's)/ Effective Time Management/ Teamwork & Teambuilding/ P.R.I.D.E- **P**ersonal **R**esponsibility **I**n **D**elivering **E**xcellence

www.ingramcontent.com/pod-product-compliance
Ingram Content Group UK Ltd.
Pitfield, Milton Keynes, MK11 3LW, UK
UKHW021340190726
13845UKWH00027B/642

9 788198 569134